GRADES 3-4

...the Super Source®

Color Tiles

ETA/Cuisenaire®
Vernon Hills, IL

ETA/Cuisenaire® extends its warmest thanks to the many teachers and students across the country who helped ensure the success of the Super Source® series by participating in the outlining, writing, and field testing of the materials.

Project Director: Judith Adams
Managing Editor: Doris Hirschhorn
Editorial Team: John Nelson, Deborah J. Slade, Harriet Slonim, Linda Dodge, Patricia Kijak Anderson
Editorial Assistant: Toni-Ann Bleecker
Field Test Coordinator: Laurie Verdeschi

Design Manager: Phyllis Aycock
Text Design: Amy Berger, Tracey Munz
Line Art and Production: Joan Lee, Fiona Santoianni
Cover Design: Michael Muldoon
Illustrations: Sean Farrell

the Super Source® Color Tiles Grades 3-4
ISBN 1-57452-001-6
ETA 015126

ETA/Cuisenaire • Vernon Hills, IL 60061-1862
800-445-5985 • www.etacuisenaire.com

Printed in the United States of America.
03 04 05 06 07 08 09 10 11   10 9 8 7 6 5 4 3

...*the Super Source*

Table of Contents

The Super Source® is a series of books, each of which contains a collection of activities to use with a specific math manipulative. Driving **the Super Source®** is our conviction that children construct their own understandings through rich, hands-on mathematical experiences. Although the activities in each book are written for a specific grade range, they all connect to the core of mathematics learning that is important to every child in grades K–6. Thus, the material in many activities can easily be refocused for children at other grade levels. Because the activities are not arranged sequentially, children can work on any activity at any time.

The lessons in **the Super Source** all follow a basic structure consistent with the vision of mathematics teaching described in the *Curriculum and Evaluation Standards for School Mathematics* published by the National Council of Teachers of Mathematics.

All of the activities in this series involve Problem Solving, Communication, Reasoning, and Mathematical Connections—the first four NCTM Standards. Each activity also focuses on one or more of the following curriculum strands: Number, Geometry, Measurement, Patterns/Functions, Probability/Statistics, Logic.

HOW LESSONS ARE ORGANIZED

At the beginning of each lesson, you will find, to the right of the title, both the major curriculum strands to which the lesson relates and the particular topics that children will work with. Each lesson has three main sections. The first, GETTING READY, offers an *Overview*, which states what children will be doing, and why, and a list of "What You'll Need." Specific numbers of Color Tiles are suggested on this list but can be adjusted as the needs of your specific situation dictate. Before an activity, tiles can be counted out and placed in containers or self-sealing plastic bags for easy distribution. When crayons are called for, it is understood that their colors match the Color Tiles and that markers may be used in place of crayons. Blackline masters that are provided for your convenience at the back of the book are referenced on this list. Paper, pencils, scissors, tape, and materials for making charts, which are necessary in certain activities, are usually not.

Although overhead Color Tiles and the suggestion to make overhead transparencies of the blackline masters are always listed in "What You'll Need" as optional, these materials are highly effective when you want to demonstrate the use of Color Tiles. As you move the tiles on the screen, children can work with the same materials at their seats. Children can also use the overhead to present their work to other members of their group or to the class.

The second section, THE ACTIVITY, first presents a possible scenario for *Introducing* the children to the activity. The aim of this brief introduction is to help you give children the tools they will need to investigate independently. However, care has been taken to avoid undercutting the activity itself. Since these investigations are designed to enable children to increase their own mathematical power, the idea is to set the stage but not steal the show! The heart of the lesson, *On Their Own*, is found in a box at the top of the second page of each lesson. Here, rich problems stimulate many different problem-solving approaches and lead to a variety of solutions. These hands-on explorations have the potential for bringing children to new mathematical ideas and deepening skills.

On Their Own is intended as a stand-alone activity for children to explore with a partner or in a small group. Be sure to make the needed directions clearly visible. You may want to write them on the chalkboard or on an overhead or present them either on reusable cards or on paper. For children who may have difficulty reading the directions, you can read them aloud or make sure that each group includes at least one "reader."

The last part of this second section, *The Bigger Picture*, gives suggestions for how children can share their work and their thinking and make mathematical connections. Class charts and children's recorded work provide a springboard for discussion. Under "Thinking and Sharing," there are several prompts that you can use to promote discussion. Children will not be able to respond to these prompts with one-word answers. Instead, the prompts encourage children to describe what they notice, tell how they found their results, and give the reasoning behind their answers. Thus children learn to verify their own results rather than relying on the teacher to determine if an answer is "right" or "wrong." Though the class discussion might immediately follow the investigation, it is important not to cut the activity short by having a class discussion too soon.

The Bigger Picture often includes a suggestion for a "Writing" (or drawing) assignment. This is meant to help children process what they have just been doing. You might want to use these ideas as a focus for daily or weekly entries in a math journal that each child keeps.

The 2X2 Square, was the hardest to keep track of because It had more blocks then the other squars. I figured it out by using the chart. I saw that 1x1 equals 1 and it was in the 6 by 6 place and 6x6 equals 36 and it was in the 1 by 1 place so I figured that the 5 by 5 answer was 2X2 and so on.

From: *Me*

Pear, Zoo
    My disin will make a better play place because. The squain gives the monkeys more room. The squain allso filles in the squains the atheor disin's left out. That's why I think my disin is better for the monkey's play place.

    Snom, Melissa

From: *Square*

The Bigger Picture always ends with ideas for "Extending the Activity." Extensions take the essence of the main activity and either alter or extend its parameters. These activities are especially appropriate for use with a class that becomes deeply involved in the primary activity or for children who finish before the others. In any case, it is probably a good idea to expose the entire class to the possibility of, and the results from, such extensions.

The third and final section of the lesson is TEACHER TALK. Here, in *Where's the Mathematics?*, you can gain insight into the underlying mathematics of the activity and discover some of the strategies children are apt to use as they work. Solutions are also given—when such are necessary and/or helpful. Because *Where's the Mathematics?* provides a view of what may happen in the lesson as well as the underlying mathematical potential that may grow out of it, this may be the section that you want to read before presenting the activity to children.

USING THE ACTIVITIES

The Super Source has been designed to fit into the variety of classroom environments in which it will be used. These range from a completely manipulative-based classroom to one in which manipulatives are just beginning to play a part. You may choose to use some activities in *the Super Source* in the way set forth in each lesson (introducing an activity to the whole class, then breaking the class up into groups that all work on the same task, and so forth). You will then be able to circulate among the groups as they work to observe and perhaps comment on each child's work. This approach requires a full classroom set of materials but allows you to concentrate on the variety of ways that children respond to a given activity.

Alternatively, you may wish to make two or three related activities available to different groups of children at the same time. You may even wish to use different manipulatives to explore the same mathematical concept. (Cuisenaire® Rods and Snap™ Cubes, for example, can be used to teach some of the same concepts as Color Tiles.) This approach does not require full classroom sets of a particular manipulative. It also permits greater adaptation of materials to individual children's needs and/or preferences.

If children are comfortable working independently, you might want to set up a "menu"— that is, set out a number of related activities from which children can choose. Children should be encouraged to write about their experiences with these independent activities.

However you choose to use *the Super Source* activities, it would be wise to allow time for several groups or the entire class to share their experiences. The dynamics of this type of interaction, in which children share not only solutions and strategies but also feelings and intuitions, is the basis of continued mathematical growth. It allows children who are beginning to form a mathematical structure to clarify it and those who have mastered just isolated concepts to begin to see how these concepts might fit together.

Again, both the individual teaching style and combined learning styles of the children should dictate the specific method of utilizing *the Super Source* lessons. At first sight, some activities may appear too difficult for some of your children, and you may find yourself tempted to actually "teach" by modeling exactly how an activity can lead to a particular learning outcome. If you do this, you rob children of the chance to try the activity in whatever way they can. As long as children have a way to begin an investigation, give them time and opportunity to see it through. Instead of making assumptions about what children will or won't do, watch and listen. The excitement and challenge of the activity—as well as the chance to work cooperatively—may bring out abilities in children that will surprise you.

If you are convinced, however, that an activity does not suit your students, adjust it, by all means. You may want to change the language, either by simplifying it or by referring to specific vocabulary that you and your children already use and are comfortable with. On the other hand, if you suspect that an activity is not challenging enough, you may want to read through the activity extensions for a variation that you can give children instead.

RECORDING

Although the direct process of working with Color Tiles is a valuable one, it is afterward, when children look at, compare, share, and think about their work, that an activity yields its greatest rewards. However, because Color Tile designs can't always be left intact, children need an effective way to record their work. To this end, at the back of this book recording paper is provided for reproduction. The "What You'll Need" listing at the beginning of each lesson often specifies the kind of recording paper to use. For example, it seems natural for children to record Color Tile patterns on grid paper. Yet it is important for children to use a method of recording that they feel comfortable with. Frustration in recording their structures can leave children feeling that the actual activity was either too difficult or just not fun! Thus, there may be times when you feel children should just share their work rather than record it.

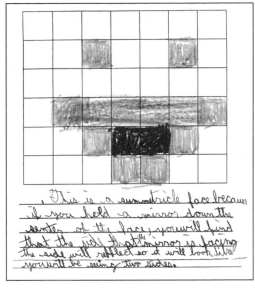

From: *How*

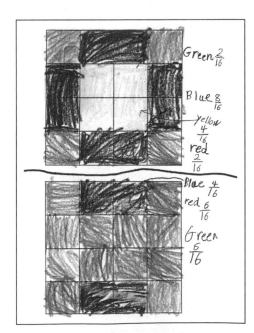

From: *Half*

Young children might duplicate their work on grid paper by coloring in boxes on grids that exactly match the tiles in size. Older children may be able to use smaller grids or even construct the recording paper as they see fit.

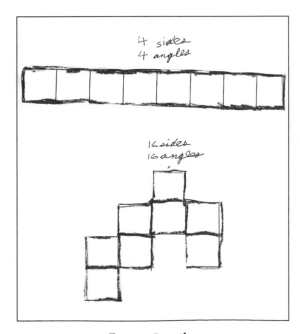

From: *Creating*

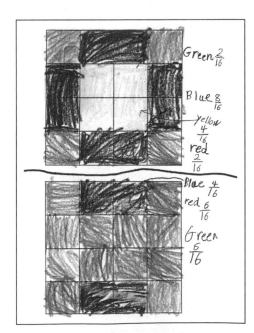

From: *Creature*

Another interesting way to "freeze" a Color Tile design is to create it using a software piece and then get a printout. Children can use a classroom or resource-room computer if it is available or, where possible, extend the activity into a home assignment by utilizing their home computers.

Recording involves more than copying designs. Writing, drawing, and making charts and tables are also ways to record. By creating a table of data gathered in the course of their investigations, children are able to draw conclusions and look for patterns. When children write or draw, either in their group or later by themselves, they are clarifying their understanding of their recent mathematical experience.

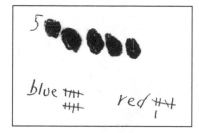

Product	Numbers rolled	Product	Numbers rolled	Product	Numbers rolled
1		13		25	
2	1×2 2×1	14		26	
3	3×1 3×1 3×1	15	5×3 3×5	27	
4	2×2	16	4×4	28	
5	5×1 1×5	17		29	
6	6×1 6×1 6×1	18	3×6 3/6	30	6×5 5×6 6×5
7		19		31	
8	4×2 4×2 2×4 2×4 4×2 3×3	20	5×4	32	
9		21		33	
10	5×2 5×2	22		34	
11		23		35	
12	4×3 3×4 6×2 2×3	24	6×4 8×4	36	

From: _Half_

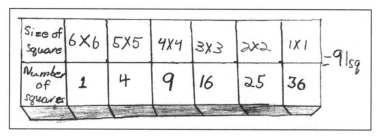

L W Number	L W Number	Number
2×1 2 Ts	12×11 132 Ts	22
3×2 6 Ts	13×12 156 Ts	24
4×3 12 Ts	14×13 182 Ts	26
5×4 20 Ts	15×14 210 Ts	28
6×5 30 Ts 10	16×15 (240 Ts)	30
7×6 42 Ts 12		
8×7 56 Ts 14		
9×8 72 Ts 16		
10×9 90 Ts 18		
11×10 110 Ts 20		

From: _Estimation_

5

blue ||||| ||||| red ||||| |

From: _Mirror_

Size of square	6×6	5×5	4×4	3×3	2×2	1×1
Number of squares	1	4	9	16	25	36

= 91 sq

From: _Very_

With a roomful of children busily engaged in their investigations, it is not easy for a teacher to keep track of how individual children are working. Having tangible material to gather and examine when the time is right will help you to keep in close touch with each child's learning.

Exploring Color Tiles

Color Tiles are a versatile collection of 1-inch square tiles that come in four colors—red, green, yellow, and blue. They are pleasant to handle and easy to manipulate. Children can use the tiles to act out story problems involving all sorts of everyday objects. Learning to use small colored squares to represent such objects is a significant step in the process of learning to abstract.

Although Color Tiles are simple in concept, they can be used to develop a wide variety of mathematical ideas at many different levels of complexity. Young children who start using Color Tiles to make patterns may be likely to talk about numbers of different-colored tiles. Some children may even spontaneously begin to count and compare numbers. The fact that the tiles are squares means that they fit naturally into a grid pattern, and when Color Tiles are used on top of a printed grid—for example, a number chart—the tiles can be used to discover many number patterns. As they record their patterns, children are also using their spatial skills and strategies to locate positions of particular tiles.

> Is there a blue between the two yellows My emportant question

From: *Last*

When making patterns, children often provide the best inspiration for one another. Given sufficient time, some child will come up with an idea that excites the imagination of other children. It is preferable that new ideas arise in this way, because then children develop confidence in their own abilities to be creative. Though children need to explore patterns freely, some children may also appreciate challenges, such as being asked to make patterns with certain types of symmetry or patterns with certain characteristics, such as specific colors that represent different fractional parts.

> I made a pattern for the first two lines and then I turned the lines around.

From: *Mirror,*

Logical thinking is always involved when children investigate Color Tile patterns, because, in order to recognize and continue a visual pattern, children must form conjectures, verify them, and then apply them.

WORKING WITH COLOR TILES

As counters, Color Tiles are very important early number models. Eventually children will develop more abstract concepts of numbers and will not be dependent on manipulation of objects. Color Tiles can help children build such abstract structures.

The tiles fall naturally into certain patterns, as shown below, and enable children to visualize the relationships as represented by the tiles.

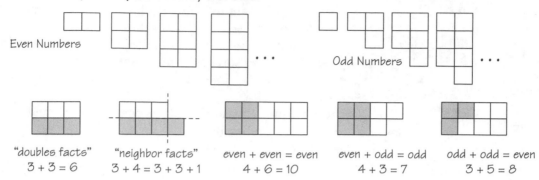

Even Numbers

Odd Numbers

"doubles facts"
3 + 3 = 6

"neighbor facts"
3 + 4 = 3 + 3 + 1

even + even = even
4 + 6 = 10

even + odd = odd
4 + 3 = 7

odd + odd = even
3 + 5 = 8

Since there are large numbers of them, Color Tiles are useful for estimation and developing number sense. Children can take a handful, estimate how many, then separate the tiles into rows of ten to identify how many "tens" and how many "ones" there are. The colors of the tiles also make them useful in developing the concept of place value. For example, children can play exchange games in which each color tile represents a place value—ones, tens, hundreds, and thousands. Exchange games can work for subtraction as well as addition, and can also refer to decimals, where tile colors would represent units, tenths, hundredths, and thousandths.

Color Tiles are very suitable for developing an understanding of the meaning of addition. The sum 2 + 3 can be modeled by taking two tiles of one color and three of another, and then counting them. Subtraction problems can also be modeled either traditionally—put up five tiles and take two away—or by taking five tiles of one color, then covering two with a different color so that it is obvious that three tiles of the original color are left. Either of these methods of modeling makes the connection between addition and subtraction apparent.

Color Tiles are also ideal for developing the concept of multiplication, both as grouping and as an array. To show 3 x 4, children can make three groups with four tiles in each group and then arrange them in a rectangular array of three rows of four tiles. The advantage of the array is that by turning it children can see that 3 x 4 = 4 x 3. The array model also leads naturally into the development of the formula for the area of the rectangle. In fact, Color Tiles are especially suitable for exploring all area and perimeter relations.

Color Tiles can be used to explore all the different ways that squares can be arranged, subject to certain constraints. One classic investigation is to find all "tetraminoes," "pentominoes," and "hexominoes," that is, all ways to arrange either four, five, or six tiles respectively, so that one complete side of each tile touches at least one complete side of another tile. Color Tiles can be used to investigate how many different rectangular arrays a given number of tiles can have. This helps children to discover that for some numbers—prime numbers—the only possible rectangular arrays are one-tile wide. At an upper-grade level, the colors of tiles can represent prime numbers, and a set of tiles can be used to represent the prime factorization of a number. For example, if a red tile represents 2 and a green tile represents 3, the number 24 might be represented by three red tiles and one green tile, since 24 = 2 x 2 x 2 x 3. This representation of numbers in terms of factors can help children to understand procedures for finding greatest common divisors and least common multiples. Since the Color Tiles all feel exactly the same, they can be used to provide hands-on experience with sampling. By using a collection of tiles in a bag, children can investigate how repeated sampling, with replacement, can be used to predict the contents of the bag. Since the tiles are square, they can also be used to represent entries in a bar graph drawn on 1-inch grid paper. For example, class opinion polls can be quickly conducted by having each child place a tile in the column on a graph which corresponds to his or her choice.

To stimulate algebraic thinking, number sentences can be introduced in which each number is covered with tiles. The challenge for children is to figure out what is under each tile. Children will learn that sometimes they can be sure of the number covered, as in $4 + \boxed{} = 6$, while at other times they cannot, as in $\boxed{} + \boxed{} = 6$. This use of tiles lays the groundwork for introducing a variable.

ASSESSING CHILDREN'S UNDERSTANDING

Color Tiles are wonderful tools for assessing children's mathematical thinking. Watching children work with their Color Tiles gives you a sense of how they approach a mathematical problem. Their thinking can be "seen," in so far as that thinking is expressed through the way they construct, recognize, and continue spatial patterns. When a class breaks up into small working groups, you are able to circulate, listen, and raise questions, all the while focusing on how individuals are thinking. Here is a perfect opportunity for authentic assessment.

Having children describe their designs and share their strategies and thinking with the whole class gives you another opportunity for observational assessment. Furthermore, you may want to gather children's recorded work or invite them to choose pieces to add to their math portfolios.

I Think it was Better To keep The Obck Together Because if There is one space in the miDDle of a square it wouID Be HarD To fill That in.

From: *Counting*

In this lesson I learned that there is no possible way no matter how many tiles you use, you can not have an odd number of sides and angles.

From: *How*

Models of teachers assessing children's understanding can be found in the series of videotapes listed below.

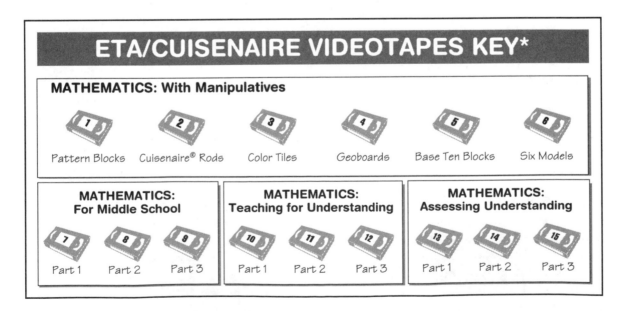

Connect
the Super Source®
to NCTM Standards.

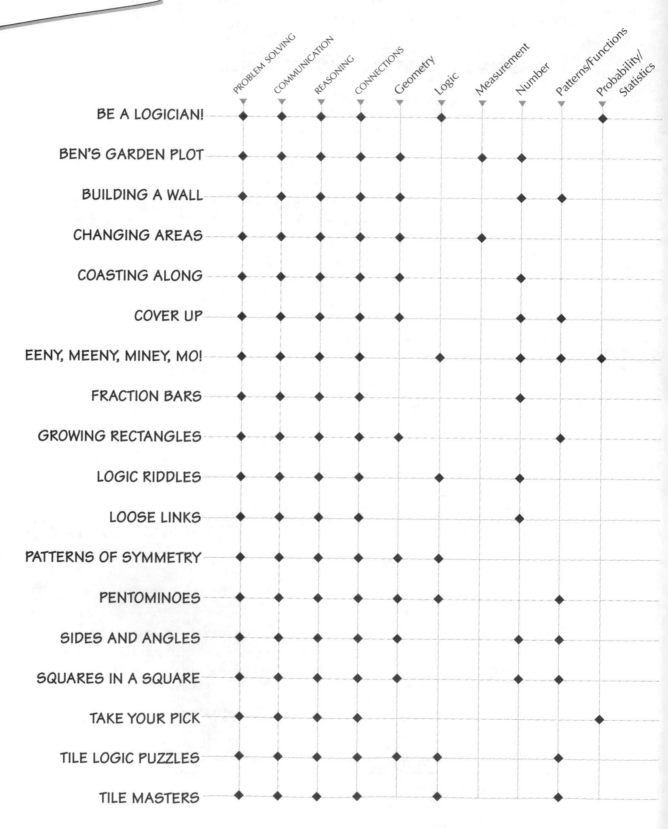

	PROBLEM SOLVING	COMMUNICATION	REASONING	CONNECTIONS	Geometry	Logic	Measurement	Number	Patterns/Functions	Probability/Statistics
BE A LOGICIAN!	◆	◆	◆	◆		◆				◆
BEN'S GARDEN PLOT	◆	◆	◆	◆	◆		◆	◆		
BUILDING A WALL	◆	◆	◆	◆				◆	◆	
CHANGING AREAS	◆	◆	◆	◆	◆		◆			
COASTING ALONG	◆	◆	◆	◆				◆		
COVER UP	◆	◆	◆	◆	◆			◆	◆	
EENY, MEENY, MINEY, MO!	◆	◆	◆	◆		◆		◆	◆	◆
FRACTION BARS	◆	◆	◆	◆				◆		
GROWING RECTANGLES	◆	◆	◆	◆	◆				◆	
LOGIC RIDDLES	◆	◆	◆	◆		◆		◆		
LOOSE LINKS	◆	◆	◆	◆						
PATTERNS OF SYMMETRY	◆	◆	◆	◆	◆		◆			
PENTOMINOES	◆	◆	◆	◆	◆	◆			◆	
SIDES AND ANGLES	◆	◆	◆	◆				◆	◆	
SQUARES IN A SQUARE	◆	◆	◆	◆	◆			◆	◆	
TAKE YOUR PICK	◆	◆	◆	◆						◆
TILE LOGIC PUZZLES	◆	◆	◆	◆	◆	◆			◆	
TILE MASTERS	◆	◆	◆	◆		◆			◆	

Correlate *the Super Source®* to your curriculum.

Addition · Area · Classifying · Comparing · Congruence · Counting · Deductive reasoning · Division · Fractions · Growth patterns · Interpreting data · Multiplication · Number sequences · Organizing data · Patterns · Perimeter · Permutations · Polygons · Predicting · Properties of numbers · Rectangles · Sampling · Sorting · Spatial visualization · Symmetry · Transformational geometry

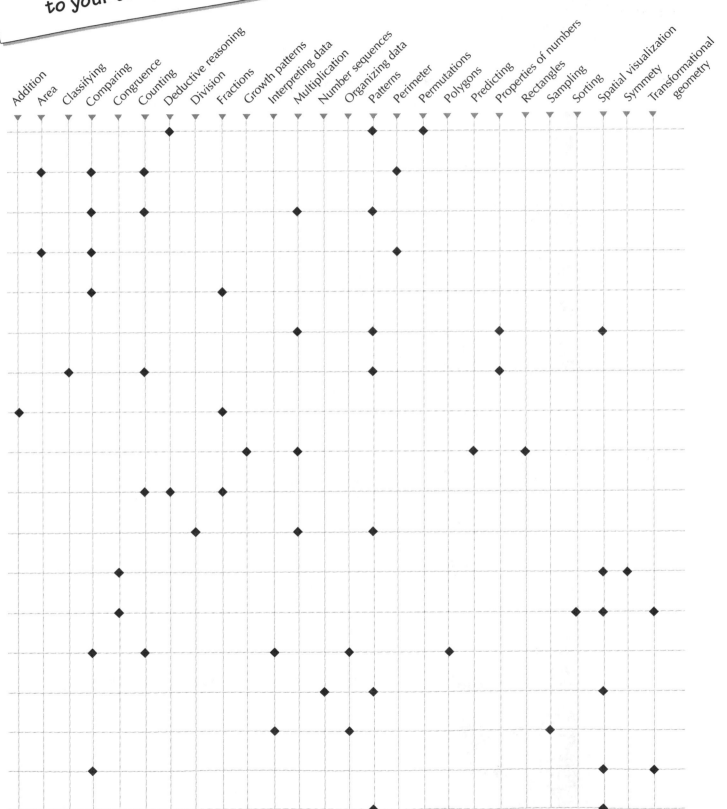

Classroom-tested activities contained in these
Super Source® Color Tiles books focus on
the math strands in the charts below.

...the Super Source® Color Tiles, Grades K-2

Geometry	Logic	Measurement
Number	Patterns/Functions	Probability/Statistics

...the Super Source® Color Tiles, Grades 5-6

Geometry	Logic	Measurement
Number	Patterns/Functions	Probability/Statistics

Classroom-tested activities contained in these *Super Source*® books focus on the math strands as indicated in these charts.

the Super Source® Base Ten Blocks, Grades 3-4

Geometry	Logic	Measurement
Number	Patterns/Functions	Probability/Statistics

the Super Source® Snap™ Cubes, Grades 3-4

Geometry	Logic	Measurement
Number	Patterns/Functions	Probability/Statistics

the Super Source® Cuisenaire® Rods, Grades 3-4

Geometry	Logic	Measurement
Number	Patterns/Functions	Probability/Statistics

the Super Source® Geoboards, Grades 3-4

Geometry	Logic	Measurement
Number	Patterns/Functions	Probability/Statistics

the Super Source® Color Tiles, Grades 3-4

Geometry	Logic	Measurement
Number	Patterns/Functions	Probability/Statistics

the Super Source® Tangrams, Grades 3-4

Geometry	Logic	Measurement
Number	Patterns/Functions	Probability/Statistics

Overview of the Lessons

See video key, page 11.

Color Tiles, Grades 3-4

 See video key, page 11.

BE A LOGICIAN!

- **Patterns**
- **Deductive reasoning**
- **Permutations**

Getting Ready

What You'll Need

Color Tiles, 1 of each color per group

Books or heavy folders to serve as barriers

Overhead Color Tiles and/or Color Tile grid paper transparency (optional)

Overview

Children use Color Tiles to play a game in which they apply logical thinking in order to guess the sequence of colors of hidden tiles. In this activity, children have the opportunity to:

- ◆ formulate hypotheses in order to satisfy conditions
- ◆ develop deductive reasoning skills

The Activity

You may want to point out that drawing the following would mean that two colors were guessed correctly with one of them in the correct position (although not necessarily in the first position).

As children offer their guesses, you may want to model the actual Color Tiles, either instead of, or in addition to, writing the letter arrangements.

Introducing

- ◆ Make a row of three Color Tiles in this order, from left to right, and keep it hidden.

- ◆ Tell children that you have hidden a row of three tiles, each of a different color. Challenge children to guess the colors of the tiles and their order—first, second, and third.

- ◆ Explain that after each guess you will write a clue on the chalkboard. For each color guessed correctly, you will draw a circle. For each position guessed correctly, you will draw a dot inside the circle.

- ◆ Call for one volunteer's guess, then record it on the chalkboard.

- ◆ Draw the appropriate clues, then ask, "What do we know from this?" You may want to keep track of guesses and responses in the way shown here.

Guess	Clues	What Do We Know?
RBG	○ ○	2 correct colors
YGR	◉ ○	2 correct colors 1 correct position
YGB	◉ ○ ○	3 correct colors 1 correct position

- ◆ Keep on calling for guesses and recording clues until the correct color and order of the tiles have been guessed.

On Their Own

Play *Be a Logician!*

Here are the rules.

1. This is a game for 4 or more players. The object is to guess the colors of 3 Color Tiles and their order, from left to right.

2. Players decide who will be the 2 Leaders and who will be the 2 Logicians.

3. The Leaders build a row of 3 Color Tiles, each tile a different color. They keep the tiles hidden from the Logicians.

4. The Logicians make guesses by naming 3 colors of tiles in order.

5. After each guess, the Leaders give a clue about how close the guess was. The clue must have 2 parts:

   • It must tell how many colors in the guess are correct.
   • It must tell how many tiles in the guess are in the correct position.

   For example, suppose the secret row of tiles was blue-green-yellow and the Logicians guessed red-green-blue. The Leaders would give this clue:
   "Two of the colors are correct, and 1 tile is in the correct position."

6. The Logicians record each guess and clue.

7. The game ends when Logicians guess the correct colors and order.

• Play several games of *Be a Logician!* Make sure that everyone in the group has a chance to be a Leader and a Logician.

• Be ready to talk about good guesses and bad guesses.

The Bigger Picture

Thinking and Sharing

As games are completed, have Logicians post their recordings of guesses and clues on the chalkboard, blocking out the last (winning) guess. Review some groups' games with the class, challenging other groups to try to supply each winning guess.

Use prompts such as these to promote class discussion:

   ◆ What was the hardest part of playing this game? What was the easiest?
   ◆ How can you describe the order of the clues given for each game?
   ◆ Which clue(s) helped you to decide which three colors were used?
   ◆ Which clue(s) helped you to decide the positions for the three colors?
   ◆ How many guesses did you need to make the winning guess?
   ◆ If you were to play the game again as a Logician, what guess(es) might you make now that you didn't make before?

Writing

Have children describe the course of play in one of the games in which they had the role of Leader.

Teacher Talk

Where's the Mathematics?

This activity gives children experience in reasoning deductively. By modeling the course of play in the *Introducing* activity, children have an opportunity to verbalize their deductive thinking and to explain their strategies. This not only helps the child doing the explaining, but it gives other children the opportunity to hear how their classmates reason.

You may want to point out that an arrangement of items in a particular order is called a *permutation*. For example, since the words *trap, tarp,* and *part* are made up of three different arrangements of the same letters, they may be thought of as being permutations of the same letters.

The *fundamental counting principle* can be used to find the number of possible permutations of a group of items. This is based on the understanding that each time an item is picked for a certain position in a permutation, one less item remains to be picked for the next position. So, the number of permutations of *n* different items is $n(n-1)(n-2)...(2)(1)$. This is written as *n!* and is read as "*n* factorial." In this activity, there are four colors and three positions. Therefore, there are four color possibilities for the first position, three for the second, and two for the third. That means that there are 4 x 3 x 2, or 24, permutations, or possible arrangements, of tiles that the Leaders can use.

The number of permutations of *n* different items, taken *r* items at a time and with no repetitions, is written as $_nP_r$. If you have a few children who are ready to see a mathematical affirmation of their findings, you may want to share this formula with them.

$$_nP_r = \frac{n!}{(n-r)!}$$

$$_4P_3 = \frac{4!}{(4-3)!}$$

$$= \frac{4 \times 3 \times 2 \times 1}{1}$$

$$= \frac{24}{1}$$

$$= 24$$

Extending the Activity

1. Ask children to list all possible solutions (permutations of four colors) in a game of *Be a Logician!* in which the four colors of tiles are used in four positions.

2. Have children play *Be a Logician!* again, this time with three Color Tiles, two of one color and one of another color.

This game is not easy, but children should improve as they get more practice. Good record keeping and an understanding of what the record means are essential for children in the Logician role. Here is the way a game could be played out using the record-keeping method shown in *Introducing*.

Hidden pattern: BGY

Guess	Clues	What Do We Know?
GRB	○○	Two colors are correct; none is in the correct position.
RBY	◉○	Two colors are correct; one of them is in the correct position. The correct colors might be R and B because they were in both guesses; but maybe G was correct and it was replaced by Y, which may be correct.
GBY	◉○○	Three colors are correct; one of them is in the correct position. R is eliminated. Since there is only one in the correct position, as in the last guess, B or Y is in the correct position.
YBG	○○○	Three colors are correct. None is in the correct position, so one was moved from a correct to an incorrect position. Looking at the last two guesses, it appears that Y was correct in the last position. Also, B can't be in the middle, so B must be first. That means that G is in the middle.
BGY	◉◉◉	That's it!

BEN'S GARDEN PLOT

- Counting
- Comparing
- Area
- Perimeter

Getting Ready

What You'll Need

Color Tiles, 30 per pair

Color Tile grid paper, several sheets per pair, page 90

Overhead Color Tiles and/or Color Tile grid paper transparency (optional)

Overview

Children use Color Tiles to design plots for a garden. In this activity, children have the opportunity to:

- ◆ find perimeter by counting
- ◆ compare shapes with the same area

The Activity

Using the edge of a tile to measure perimeter is a way for children to keep from making counting errors.

Introducing

- ◆ Display this design and ask children to build it with eight Color Tiles.

- ◆ Tell children that you can find the distance around this design by using another Color Tile. Hold a tile on edge and demonstrate how to use it to measure part way around the design.

- ◆ Ask children to finish measuring on their own. Confirm that the distance around is 14 units.

- ◆ Point out that if this were a design for a fenced-in garden, the garden would need to have 14 units of fencing.

On Their Own

How can you help Ben to design a fenced-in garden in which he can plant 10 kinds of vegetables?

- With a partner, make different designs for Ben's garden. Use 10 Color Tiles for each design.

- Each tile in a design must touch at least 1 other tile along a complete side.

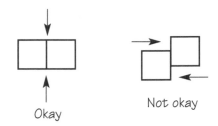

Okay   Not okay

- Record your designs.

- Find how much fencing Ben will need for each design by measuring around it with the edge of another Color Tile. Write that number next to the design.

- Choose the design that you like best and cut it out.

The Bigger Picture

Thinking and Sharing

Ask pairs of children how much fencing they would need for their cutout design. Begin a chalkboard graph by labeling columns with the least number mentioned. Ask children with a design requiring that amount of fencing to post it in that column. Invite children with different designs requiring that amount of fencing to post them in the same column. Continue this process until all the designs are posted in the appropriate columns.

If all the posted designs for a particular number are the same, suggest that children look through their drawings to find a different design to post.

Use prompts like these to promote class discussion:

- Which column has the most designs? the fewest?

- How many more designs are there with a fencing of ——— than with a fencing of ———? Explain how you know.

- How many fewer designs are there with a fencing of ——— than with a fencing of ———? Explain how you know.

- What do you notice as you look at all the designs on the graph?

- What is the same about all the designs? What is different?

- Which design do you think Ben would pick for his garden? Why?

Drawing and Writing

Ask children to draw their favorite garden-plot design for Ben. Then have them write a note to Ben explaining why he should pick their plot design.

Teacher Talk

Where's the Mathematics?

In addition to counting and comparing, this activity gives children the opportunity to make observations that relate to several important geometry and measurement ideas. One is that although all their garden plots have 10 tiles each, the plots do not all require the same amount of fencing. Noticing this lays the groundwork for understanding the concept that not all shapes with the same area have the same perimeter.

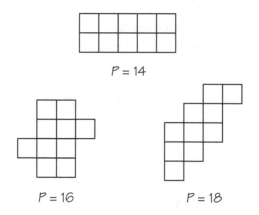

Another observation that children may make, especially as they study the postings, is that garden plots with the same number of tiles and the same distance around do not always look alike; that is, different shapes can have the same area and the same perimeter.

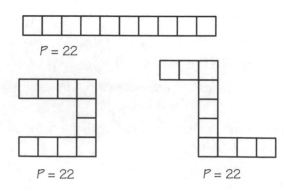

There are five possible perimeters for a 10-tile design: 14, 16, 18, 20, and 22. Some of the possible designs are shown on the next page.

Extending the Activity

1. Have children repeat the activity, this time changing the number of tiles to design a garden for a different number of vegetables.

2. Have children sort their designs in new ways: number of sides, symmetrical or not, long and skinny, or short and fat.

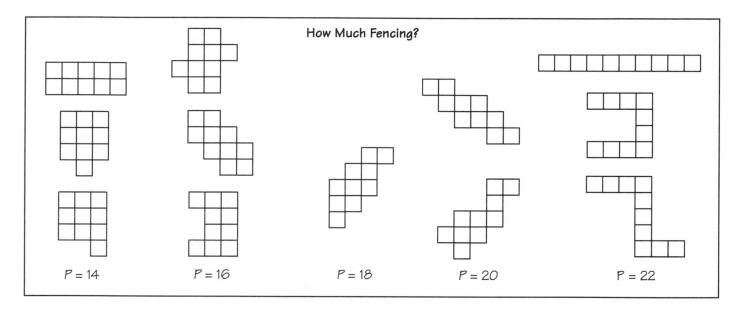

How Much Fencing?

P = 14   P = 16   P = 18   P = 20   P = 22

Children do not instinctively realize how placing tiles side by side affects the perimeter of a shape. It is a difficult idea for young children to understand that every time a side of a tile touches another, two sides are no longer part of the perimeter. With experience, children can discover that the number of exposed sides of a tile decreases from four to zero as new tiles are added.

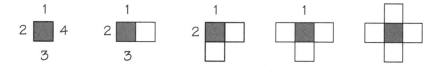

Posting children's work as suggested forms a *How Much Fencing?* graph like the one shown above. Such a graph provides a structure that helps children analyze the data. Posting the actual shapes is visually powerful, whereas non-pictorial recording techniques such as tally marks or checks limit the activity to a numerical discussion.

Children will have different ideas about which plot Ben would choose for his garden. Some may like the ones that show symmetry or some sort of design. Others may point out that the more compact designs might fit better in a family's yard. Still others may recommend the long, skinny plots because with these, Ben would not have to step on other parts of the plot when he does chores such as weeding.

BUILDING A WALL

- Counting
- Comparing
- Patterns
- Multiplication

Getting Ready

What You'll Need

Color Tiles, about 40 each of red and blue per pair

Color Tile grid paper, several sheets per pair, page 90

Crayons

Tape

Overhead Color Tiles and/or Color Tile grid paper transparency (optional)

Overview

Children create a two-color pattern for a Color Tile wall. They extend the pattern, then determine how many tiles would be needed to repeat the pattern a given number of times. In this activity, children have the opportunity to:

- ◆ connect visual patterns to numerical patterns
- ◆ organize and record data
- ◆ use patterns to make predictions

Number of Blue Tiles	Total Number of Tiles
1	3
2	6
3	

The Activity

If some children find it too difficult to stand the tiles up on end, suggest that they build a path instead of a wall, laying the tiles flat rather than standing them up.

Introducing

- ◆ Show children this wall made by standing red and blue Color Tiles on end. Ask them to copy it with their Color Tiles.

R	B	R	B	R	B	R	B

- ◆ Establish that the basic pattern in the wall consists of two different colors of tiles that repeat.

- ◆ Ask how many tiles there are of each color and how many tiles there are in all.

- ◆ Then have children use their Color Tiles to copy this basic pattern for a wall.

B	R	R

- ◆ Ask volunteers to predict how many tiles of each color there would be if this pattern were repeated until there was a total of nine tiles.

- ◆ Have children extend their walls to check their predictions.

On Their Own

Can you figure out the number of red and blue Color Tiles you will need to make a wall that is 10 patterns long?

- Work with a partner. Use red and blue Color Tiles to make a pattern for a wall. A pattern has 2 or more tiles of different colors in a particular order.

- When you have agreed on your pattern, stand up the tiles to look like a real wall.

- Use Color Tiles to make walls that are 1 pattern long, 2 patterns long, and so on up to 5 patterns long.

- Record each wall on a strip of grid paper. You may need to tape some of the strips together.

- For each wall, record the number of red tiles used, the number of blue tiles used, and the total number of tiles used.

- Look for patterns in your data. Predict how many tiles of each color you will need and how many tiles you will need altogether to make a wall that is 10 patterns long. Write down your prediction.

- Now check your prediction by completing your 10-pattern wall.

- Look for a way to make predictions for even longer walls.

- Be ready to discuss any number patterns you found in your data.

The Bigger Picture

Thinking and Sharing

Invite pairs of children to post their results.

Use prompts such as these to promote class discussion:

- How do these basic wall patterns differ from each other?
- What number patterns did you find in your data?
- If you know the number of red tiles in a wall, how could you find the total number of tiles in the wall?
- If you know the total number of tiles in a wall, how could you find the number of red tiles?
- If this wall had 100 tiles, how could you find the number of blue tiles?
- How could you find the number of red tiles, blue tiles, and tiles in all if this pattern were repeated 100 times?

Writing

Ask children to imagine that their wall continued on and on. Have them explain how they could find the total number of tiles in the wall for any number of red tiles you name.

Teacher Talk

Where's the Mathematics?

By creating their basic two-color pattern, then repeating it to build their wall, children become aware that patterns repeat in predictable ways. Some children may have difficulty identifying the basic patterns in the walls built by others. This may be due either to faulty repetition of the patterns themselves or to children's inability to visually isolate a part from a whole. If the latter is the case, it might be helpful to lead children in "reading" some wall patterns aloud, pausing between the repetitions of the patterns. For example, to help children identify the basic pattern in the wall shown here, you might lead children in chanting, "blue, blue, red, blue, red"; (pause) "blue, blue, red, blue, red"; (pause) "blue, blue, red, blue, red"; (pause) "blue, blue, red, blue, red"; (pause) "blue, blue, red, blue, red."

This chart shows an example of the data that children might come up with. With data organized in this fashion, children may be able to predict the number of tiles of each color and the number of tiles in all, in the tenth pattern without actually extending the wall that far.

Number of pattern	Number of red tiles	Number of blue tiles	Total number of tiles
1st	2	3	5
2nd	4	6	10
3rd	6	9	15
4th	8	12	20
5th	10	15	25

Extending the Activity

Have pairs create wall patterns with three colors of tiles. Have them extend their walls for several patterns. Then ask them to write a few sentences that describe their walls without identifying the actual pattern. Direct pairs to exchange descriptions of their walls, then work together to build each other's walls from the descriptions.

Children who recognize the sequence of patterns as shown in the second, third, and fourth columns—counting by twos, threes, and fives—may continue the numerical patterns to conclude that by the end of the tenth pattern, there will be 20 red tiles and 30 blue tiles for a total of 50 tiles. Some children will simply double all the numbers for the fifth patterns and wind up with the data for the tenth. From this data, children could also work backward to determine that if a wall made from this pattern were 100 tiles long (4 x 25), it would need to have 60 blue tiles (4 x 15).

Some children may need to extend their data tables to find the numbers of tiles of each color and tiles in all in 100 patterns. Others may realize that they can merely multiply the number of each color and the number of tiles in all contained in one pattern by 100 to find the solution.

Those children with a more highly developed understanding of patterning will sense that the ratio of the numbers of tiles within a pattern remains constant for any number of repetitions of the patterns. They may also be able to identify other number relationships, noting, for example, that the difference between the number of red and blue tiles (blue minus red) is equal to the pattern number. Noticing all this, a child may realize that, for the hundredth pattern, the difference between the numbers of red and blue tiles must be a number whose difference is 100 and that the total number of tiles must be 10 times the total number of the tenth pattern.

Number of pattern	Number of red tiles	Number of blue tiles	Total number of tiles
10th	20	30	50
100th	200	300	500

CHANGING AREAS

- **Perimeter**
- **Area**
- **Comparing**

Getting Ready

What You'll Need

Color Tiles, 50 per pair

Color Tile grid paper, several sheets per pair, page 90

Crayons

Color Tile writing paper, page 91 (optional)

Overhead Color Tiles and/or Color Tile grid paper transparency (optional)

Overview

Children build a Color Tile shape, then find its perimeter. They build other shapes with the same perimeter, then find the area of each of these shapes. In this activity, children have the opportunity to:

- ◆ measure to find the perimeter of a shape
- ◆ develop the understanding that figures with the same perimeter can have different areas

The Activity

You may wish to review that the perimeter of a shape is the measure of the distance around it and that the area of a shape is the number of square units needed to completely cover it.

Introducing

- ◆ Display this shape made from Color Tiles of one color. Have children copy it.
- ◆ Show children how to move the edge of another Color Tile around the shape to measure its perimeter.
- ◆ Have a volunteer give the perimeter. Confirm that the perimeter may be expressed as 10 units or 10 inches (10 in.).
- ◆ Have another volunteer give the area. Confirm that the area may be expressed as 4 square units or 4 square inches (4 in.^{2}).
- ◆ Ask children to use four more Color Tiles to make a different shape in which each tile touches at least one other tile along a complete side. Have children find the perimeter and the area of their shape and share the results.

On Their Own

How many different Color Tile shapes can you make that have the same perimeter?

- Work with a partner. Use 3 to 8 Color Tiles to make a shape. Each tile in the shape must touch at least 1 other tile along a complete side.

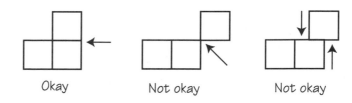

Okay   Not okay   Not okay

- Record your shape.

- Find the perimeter of your shape and write it above the recording.

- Now use Color Tiles to make as many different shapes as you can that have the same perimeter. Record each shape and its area.

- Be ready to talk about how you made shapes with the same perimeter and what you learned about their areas.

The Bigger Picture

Thinking and Sharing

Write the heading *Perimeters* at the top of the chalkboard. Ask volunteers to announce the number of units (or inches) in the perimeters of their figures. As children respond, list the perimeters across the chalkboard in ascending order. Then call out the perimeters, allowing pairs with shapes having the given perimeters to post their recordings below each one.

Use prompts such as these to promote class discussion:

- What do you notice about the posted shapes?

- How many different values for the area did you find?

- After you made your first shape, how did you go about making different shapes with the same perimeter?

- Do you see any patterns among your shapes? Explain.

- Do you notice a relationship between shapes with the same perimeter and the areas of those shapes? Explain.

Drawing and Writing

Tell children to imagine that a zoo needs help designing a play area for monkeys. Children can help by making a design with a perimeter of 36 units (or yards) of fencing. Direct children to use Color Tiles to make their designs. Then have them record the design that gives the monkeys the most room to play. Children can write a note to the zoo telling why their design would make a good play area for monkeys.

Extending the Activity

Challenge children to build two Color Tile shapes, one with a perimeter of 20 units (or inches) and having the least possible area and the other with the same perimeter and having the greatest possible area.

Teacher Talk

Where's the Mathematics?

Some children believe that the area and perimeter of shapes are always consistent with each other. Such children might think, for example, that if one shape with a perimeter of 14 inches has an area of 6 square inches, then all shapes with a perimeter of 14 inches have an area of 6 square inches. In this activity, children discover that this is not necessarily true.

To help children keep from counting the same edge of a shape more than once, you may want to show them how to place a finger at their starting point, giving this edge the count of "one."

Children are often introduced to the concept of area with models of rectangular arrays used to demonstrate multiplication. Thus, they may have an understanding of area that is limited to the terms of the formula "area equals length times width." By counting to find the area of each irregular shape they build in this activity, children can expand their understanding of area as "the number of square units that cover a region."

It will be evident from the postings that for most of the perimeters, many different shapes can be made. One way children might approach this activity is by examining the number of sides that each tile contributes to the perimeter of the shape. For example, they may notice that a tile with just one edge matching an adjacent tile has three exposed sides that contribute 3 inches to the perimeter of a shape. Likewise, a tile with two edges matching other tiles contributes 2 inches to the perimeter.

Some children may make their first shape by simply forming a row of Color Tiles. After finding the perimeter of this shape, they may come to realize that to change it into a different shape with the same perimeter, they could shorten it, reposition the extra tiles, and perhaps add more tiles. Consider the following scenario in which a pair of children built their first shape, then modified it incrementally, each time maintaining the perimeter of the first shape.

1. The pair began with this shape.

P = 14 units

2. They moved one tile in their first shape into another position.

P = 14 units

3. They added another tile in a strategic position to their second shape so that 2 units of perimeter were lost and 2 units were gained.

P = 14 units

4. They changed the third shape by adding another tile below the third tile in the top row.

P = 14 units

5. They changed the fourth shape by moving the first tile in the top row to the bottom right, thus creating two rows of 4 tiles.

P = 14 units

Once having focused on creating multiple shapes with a single perimeter, children will turn to identifying the area of each of these shapes. The pair that created the shapes in the example above, although aware of having used the same number of tiles in their first and second shapes, lost track of the fact that they added a tile to produce their third shape, then added another tile to produce their fourth and fifth shapes. Ultimately, this pair learned that their shapes, all with a perimeter of 14 units, could have areas of 6 square units, 7 square units, and 8 square units, and realized that shapes with a constant perimeter do not necessarily have a constant area.

COASTING ALONG

Getting Ready

What You'll Need

Color Tiles, about 25 per child

4 x 4 Color Tile grids, 1 sheet per child, page 92

Crayons

Color Tile writing paper, 1 sheet per pair, page 91

Overhead Color Tiles and/or Color Tile grid paper transparency (optional)

Overview

Children use Color Tiles to design square coasters. They record their designs, then determine the fractional part of the whole that each color represents. In this activity, children have the opportunity to:

◆ create patterns

◆ identify fractional parts of a whole

◆ work with equivalent fractions

The Activity

Introducing

◆ Display this square arrangement of Color Tiles. Ask children to tell what fraction of the whole square each color represents.

Y	G
B	R

◆ Elicit that each color represents 1 out of 4, or one fourth (1/4), of the whole square.

◆ Now build this square of just two colors and have children copy it.

B	B
G	G

◆ Ask volunteers to name the fractional part of the whole square that is blue and the fractional part that is green.

◆ Change the arrangement of the colors in the two-color square and have children do the same. With each change, have children identify the fractional part that each color represents.

G	G
B	B

B	G
G	B

G	B
B	G

◆ Elicit that for all the two-color squares, the fractional part of each color represents the same part of the whole no matter how the four tiles are arranged.

On Their Own

> ### How can you use Color Tiles to make a design for a square coaster?
>
> - Choose any 16 Color Tiles. Arrange them to form a square coaster design with 4 tiles on a side. You may change colors and arrangements until you have a design you like.
>
> - Record your coaster design.
>
> - On the back of your recording, list the colors you used. Next to each, write the fraction that stands for the part of the whole design that the color represents. For example, if your design had 7 red tiles and 9 blue tiles, you would write this on the back of your design:
>
>   red: $\frac{7}{16}$ blue: $\frac{9}{16}$
>
> - Exchange design recordings with a classmate. (Don't peek at the backs!) Write a fraction for each color in your classmate's design. Then check the back of that design to see if you both wrote the same fractions. Discuss the results.
>
> - Be ready to tell how to figure out the fractional parts of a coaster design.

The Bigger Picture

Thinking and Sharing

Have volunteers post their coaster designs. You may wish to have the postings grouped according to predominating colors, similar designs, or like fractional parts.

Use prompts like these to promote class discussion:

- What words can you use to describe the coaster design you made?

- Are any of the posted designs exactly alike? Are any almost alike? How?

- Would any of the posted designs become exactly alike if some of the colors were exchanged? Explain.

- Which design is made up of one half of a color? Which is made up of one quarter of a color? one eighth of a color? one sixteenth of a color?

- Which four designs do you think could be put together to make a set of four coasters? Why do you think so?

Drawing and Writing

Working in pairs, have children come to an agreement on four designs for a set of four coasters. Have children copy the designs, then tell why they decided to put these four together.

Extending the Activity

1. Have children make as many 16-tile square designs as they can that are $\frac{1}{4}$ red and $\frac{3}{4}$ yellow.

2. Challenge children to design a 16-tile square coaster made up of these fractional parts: $\frac{3}{8}$ blue, $\frac{4}{8}$ red, and $\frac{2}{16}$ yellow.

Where's the Mathematics?

With four colors to choose from, children will create a great variety of 16-tile coaster designs. What is most important is that they first build their designs so that they find them pleasing, then later, determine the fractional parts that make up the whole.

Many children will make their designs from all four colors of tiles. Yet others may use three colors, two colors, or even just one color! A "design" of a single color provides children with the opportunity to strengthen and/or share their understanding of the fact that a single fraction can be equal to a whole. The child who makes an all-green design, for example, might write this on the back of the recording: green: *16/16 = 1*.

Children lacking an understanding of equivalent fractions may be able to identify the tiles of each color only as a number of sixteenths. The following recording is an example of such a case:

Y	B	B	B
B	Y	B	B
B	B	Y	B
B	B	B	Y

blue: 12/16
yellow: 4/16

An important part of this activity is the follow-up interchange between children who have exchanged recordings and have identified the fractional parts of one another's design. At this point, the child who produced the recording above is confronted with another child having identified the colors in the design as being blue: 3/4, yellow: 1/4. Thus, the first child becomes aware that 12/16 is equivalent to 3/4 and that 4/16 is equivalent to 1/4.

To drive home this point, you might need to copy a child's design, then with the child looking on, regroup the tiles according to color. For example, regrouping the tiles in the design above may help children more readily see that since each group of four makes up one quarter of the whole of sixteen, one quarter is yellow and three quarters are blue.

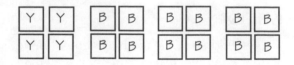

Similarly, regrouping the tiles of the design into eight groups of two can help children see that two eighths are yellow and six eighths are blue.

The criteria for making groups of four designs to form a "set of coasters" will vary. Children may suggest grouping designs according to the similarity of the way they look and/or the colors used.

Each design is the same as the others, except for color.

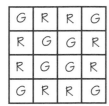

G	R	R	G
R	G	G	R
R	G	G	R
G	R	R	G

Y	G	G	Y
G	Y	Y	G
G	Y	Y	G
Y	G	G	Y

R	Y	Y	R
Y	R	R	Y
Y	R	R	Y
R	Y	Y	R

B	G	G	B
G	B	B	G
G	B	B	G
B	G	G	B

Each design is red and one other color.

B	R	R	B
R	R	R	R
R	R	R	R
B	R	R	B

R	R	R	R
R	Y	R	Y
R	R	R	R
Y	R	Y	R

R	R	R	R
R	B	B	R
R	B	B	R
R	R	R	R

R	G	R	G
G	R	G	R
R	G	R	G
G	R	G	R

Some children may group designs according to like numbers of fractional parts of a certain color. A pair in one class agreed that the following four designs would make a good set because, they noted, "Half of each of these designs is blue."

Each design is 1/2 blue.

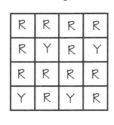

R	R	B	B
R	R	B	B
B	B	R	R
B	B	R	R

Y	B	Y	B
B	R	B	R
R	B	R	B
B	Y	B	Y

B	Y	Y	B
R	B	B	R
R	B	B	R
B	Y	Y	B

G	B	G	B
G	B	G	B
G	B	G	B
G	B	G	B

A few children may group sets according to their like numbers of fractional parts of a color regardless of the actual color of each.

Each design is 1/8 of one color and 3/8 of another color.

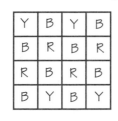

B	Y	Y	Y
Y	R	B	B
B	B	R	Y
Y	Y	Y	B

G	Y	Y	B
Y	R	R	B
B	R	R	Y
B	Y	Y	G

G	B	G	G
R	R	R	G
G	R	R	R
G	G	B	G

G	B	G	R
Y	B	R	B
B	R	B	Y
R	G	B	G

COVER UP

- **Multiplication**
- **Spatial visualization**
- **Patterns**
- **Properties of numbers**

Getting Ready

What You'll Need

Color Tiles, 100 of mixed colors per child

5 x 5 Color Tile grids,* 4 per child, page 93

Cover-Up Product List, page 94

Dice, 1 pair per group

Tape

Overhead Color Tiles and/or Color Tile grid paper transparency (optional)

Overview

In this game for two to four players, children build Color Tile arrays to cover squares on a hundreds board according to a roll of a pair of dice. In this activity, children have the opportunity to:

- ◆ create arrays to represent products
- ◆ use the commutative property of multiplication
- ◆ use the distributive property
- ◆ look for patterns in the rolls of a pair of dice

The Activity

Some children may break up their arrays in ways that fail to maintain the factors. In the example at the right, showing the product 12 by reorganizing the array into two rows of six would not be acceptable.

*Have children create their 10-by-10 game boards by cutting out four 5 x 5 grids and taping them together to form a square configuration.

Introducing

- ◆ Tell children that you rolled a pair of dice and that 4 and 3 came up. Show them how to model the outcome 4 x 3 with a Color Tile array of four rows with three tiles in each row.

4 x 3

- ◆ Ask children to use their Color Tiles to model the outcome as 3 x 4 using three rows with four tiles in each row.

3 x 4

- ◆ Show children some ways to break up the first array into individual factors consisting of rows of tiles.

For 4 x 3, 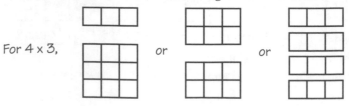 or ... or ...

- ◆ Have children show ways to break up the second array into factors.

On Their Own

Play *Cover Up!*

Here are the rules:

1. This is a game for 2 to 4 players. The object is to be the first to completely cover a 10-by-10 game board with Color Tiles.

2. Each player gets a game board. All players share a list of products from 1 to 36. After each roll of the dice, players write the 2 numbers rolled next to the product of those numbers. For example, if a player rolls a 3 and a 4, that player would write 3 x 4 next to the product 12 on the list.

3. Players take turns rolling the dice and making a Color Tile array to place on their game boards. Examples of arrays for 3 and 4 are shown to the right.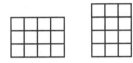

4. If a whole array does not fit, a player may break it up into parts. The parts must show the numbers rolled.

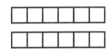

Okay for 4 x 3 or 3 x 4   Not okay for 4 x 3 or 3 x 4

5. Any player who rolls numbers for which no array will fit loses a turn.

6. The winner is the player who completely covers his or her board first.

- Play several games of *Cover Up*.
- Be ready to talk about your games and strategies.

The Bigger Picture

Thinking and Sharing

Invite children to talk about their games and describe some of the thinking they did.

Use prompts like these to promote class discussion:

- Did the arrays for some numbers fit more easily than others? Why?
- When your board began to fill up, which number pairs did you want to roll? Explain.
- Which products from 1 through 36 could you never roll? Why?
- Were some products rolled more often than others? Which ones? Do you think this would happen if you played again? Explain.
- Which was better, leaving "holes" on the board between your arrays or keeping your arrays close together? Why?

Writing

Ask children to imagine that they are about to play *Cover Up* again. Have them explain what they think is the most important thing to do in order to fill their game board as quickly as possible.

Where's the Mathematics?

Children gain practice in applying the properties of multiplication as they decide how to make or break up their Color Tile arrays to fit on their game boards. They employ the commutative property of multiplication as they consider which way to represent each product. Most children will discover that it is usually better to use the smaller number rolled as the number of tiles per row. For example, a child who rolls 4 and 6 for a product of 24 will find that making six rows of four tiles will likely provide more fitting options than would making four rows of six. However, there are times—perhaps at the beginning of the game—when four rows of six would fit nicely. Here are some of the ways that six rows of four tiles can be broken up.

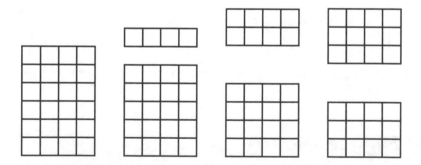

As children break up their arrays, positioning the parts wherever they fit on their boards, they are employing the distributive property of multiplication.

Extending the Activity

Have a pair of children play this version of *Cover Up* using a 10-by-10 game board and just two colors of tiles: The first player chooses a color and makes arrays in that color when he or she rolls products through 18. (Rolling a product greater that 18 loses a turn.) The second player uses the other color to show only the products from 20 through 36. (Rolling a product less than 20 loses a turn.) If both players, in succession, roll a product that cannot fit on the board, the game ends. The winner is the player who has covered the greater number of spaces on the board.

Children will come to realize that not all the products from 1 to 36 can be rolled and that some products will come up more often than others because there are more ways to roll them. This is shown in the chart on the right. Children will be surprised to note that 18, or half, of the numbers in their product list can never be rolled!

As a game progresses, the way in which the empty squares on a board are configured is also a significant factor. The two grids below each have 32 empty spaces.

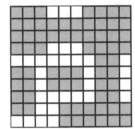

This player loses a turn by rolling 6,6; 6,5; 6,4; or 5,5.

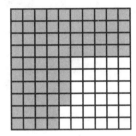

This player loses a turn only by rolling 6,6.

Through comparing game boards that look like these, children will note that it is better to fill the boards tightly rather than leaving "holes."

Product	Factors
1	1 x 1
2	1 x 2, 2 x 1
3	1 x 3, 3 x 1
4	1 x 4, 4 x 1, 2 x 2
5	1 x 5, 5 x 1
6	1 x 6, 6 x 1, 2 x 3, 3 x 2
7	—
8	2 x 4, 4 x 2
9	3 x 3
10	2 x 5, 5 x 2
11	—
12	2 x 6, 6 x 2, 3 x 4, 4 x 3
13	—
14	—
15	3 x 5, 5 x 3
16	4 x 4
17	—
18	3 x 6, 6 x 3
19	—
20	4 x 5, 5 x 4
21	—
22	—
23	—
24	4 x 6, 6 x 4
25	5 x 5
26	—
27	—
28	—
29	—
30	5 x 6, 6 x 5
31	—
32	—
33	—
34	—
35	—
36	6 x 6

EENY, MEENY, MINEY, MO!

- Counting
- Classifying
- Properties of numbers
- Patterns

Getting Ready

What You'll Need

Color Tiles, 12 per pair

Color Tile grid paper, page 90

Overhead Color Tiles and/or Color Tile grid paper transparency (optional)

Overview

Children count on Color Tiles as they chant a counting rhyme in order to work through an elimination process. In this activity, children have the opportunity to:

◆ model a familiar activity, recognizing that it involves mathematics

◆ gather data

◆ look for patterns in the data

◆ develop strategic and logical thinking

The Activity

You may wish to point very deliberately to one child on each count to make children aware that there are sixteen counts in this rhyme:

Eeny, |meeny, |miney, |mo!
Catch a |rabbit |by the |toe.
If he |hollers, |let him |go.
Eeny, |meeny, |miney, |mo!

Introducing

◆ Ask children to share ways of deciding who goes first in a game.

◆ Call for three volunteers to pretend they are going to play a game. Line them up and say that the class will help them choose who will go first.

◆ Point first to the left-most volunteer, then to each of the others in turn on each count, as the class together chants "Eeny, Meeny, Miney, Mo!"

◆ When the rhyme ends, explain that the child to whom you are now pointing is eliminated, or "out."

◆ Ask children how many more times you must chant the rhyme in order to find out who will go first. Elicit that one more round is needed.

◆ Chant the rhyme again. Establish that to choose from among three children, it takes two rounds of the rhyme.

◆ Ask children if they think there is a way to predict who would be out in each round if you chose for first again, this time with three other children.

On Their Own

Can you use Color Tiles and a rhyme to predict who will go first in games with different numbers of players?

- Work with a partner. Try this way of choosing who goes first in a game.

  - Each of you pick a number, 1 or 2. Place 2 Color Tiles on a grid and number them 1 and 2.

  - Say this rhyme together and count the tiles back and forth starting with tile 1. The counting places in the rhyme are underlined.

  - The last tile counted is "out." That means that the player whose tile is left goes first.

  > Eeny, meeny, miney, mo!
  > Catch a rabbit by the toe.
  > If he hollers, let him go.
  > Eeny, meeny, miney, mo!

- Record your results by writing down the number of players, the number of times you had to say the rhyme, and the number of the player who goes first.

- Now use this choosing process to decide who will go first when there are 3 players, 4 players, 5 players, and so on up to 12 players. When a player is counted out, begin counting with the next player in line.

- Record your findings for each number of players.

- Look for patterns in your results. Be ready to talk about how you got your results.

The Bigger Picture

Thinking and Sharing

Help children compare their results by having them complete a class chart with the column headings: *Number of players (color tiles); Number of rounds needed; Number of player (color tile) chosen to be first.*

Use prompts such as these to promote class discussion:

- How did you use the Color Tiles to solve the problem?

- In the first round of the rhyme, which word stands for the fourth player? the eighth? the twelfth? the sixteenth?

- How many rounds of the rhyme did you need for each number of players?

- In which position would you stand if you wanted to go first in a game with four players? with six players? with twelve players?

- In which position might you stand if you did *not* want to be chosen to go first in a game with five players? with eight players? with eleven players?

- Did you find any patterns in your data? Explain.

Writing

Have children explain why they think that using the "Eeny, Meeny, Miney, Mo!" rhyme to choose for first is either fair or unfair.

Teacher Talk

Where's the Mathematics?

Most children and many adults think of using counting rhymes as a way of assuring a random, or "fair," selection. This activity helps children to see that much of what happens in these situations is not random at all but is instead mathematically predictable. Through this understanding, children learn how they can use mathematics to their advantage.

"Eeny, Meeny, Miney, Mo!" is chanted in sixteen beats. Some children will always begin by counting themselves first (as the "Eeny" player). Others may begin differently, usually by counting a person next to them. While this does not really matter mathematically, what does matter is that the "Eeny" player (or Color Tile) is always recorded as "1."

Children may find this activity very challenging, and so they may do better working in groups of three or four instead of in pairs. You may also have them find data through only four or five players instead of through twelve.

Some children may position their tiles in a row on Color Tile grid paper, numbering them, one for each player. At the end of each round, they may cross out the tile that is eliminated. Other children may arrange their Color Tiles in a circle to show how people usually stand when choosing. The class might decide to choose one color for the first ("Eeny") tile, another color for even-numbered tiles, and a third color for odd-numbered tiles.

A few children will discover that they do not need to repeat the rhyme again and again in order to collect data but can instead count to 16 each time. They may even find that they do not need to count all the way to 16 each time but may instead count up from the number of tiles left in the group. For example, if seven Color Tiles remain from the previous round, they may realize that they can start the counting for the next round by counting the next tile as "8," then counting on to 16.

Extending the Activity

Have children repeat the activity using other rhymes of their choosing. Help children identify the number of counts in each. Ask children whether they think one of these rhymes might be better to use for choosing than "Eeny, Meeny, Miney, Mo!" Have them explain their reasoning.

Number of Players (Color Tiles)	Number of Rounds Needed	Number of Player (Color Tile) Chosen to Be First
2	1	1
3	2	2
4	3	2
5	4	3
6	5	1
7	6	3
8	7	3
9	8	1
10	9	7
11	10	1
12	11	5

As they look for patterns in their data, children may note that except for the number 2 player (or tile), all those chosen to be first are odd numbered. They may want to see if this pattern holds with even greater numbers of players. If time allows, children should be encouraged to extend the investigation to see if this pattern continues.

Children will find that the number of elimination rounds needed to make a final choice is one less than the number of tiles in a given group. You may want to point out, for example, that nine people in a group means that eight elimination rounds are needed. You might use this as a way to create and experiment with a simple formula:

$$\text{Round Number} = \text{Group Number} - 1$$
$$R = G - 1$$

It will probably become clear to most children that if they do not want to be chosen first, they should stand in an even-numbered position (relative to the "Eeny" player or tile number 1) but not beside that player in the counting order. Children will also probably notice that knowing where the counting starts is essential to predicting the outcome.

FRACTION BARS

Getting Ready

What You'll Need

Color Tiles, 25 of mixed colors per pair

Color Tile grid paper, page 90

Crayons

Overhead Color Tiles and/or Color Tile grid paper transparency (optional)

Overview

Children use Color Tiles to build a fraction bar that represents a whole. They write a set of clues to enable others to build the fraction bar. In this activity, children have the opportunity to:

◆ develop a model for fractions

◆ use fraction notation

◆ work with equivalent fractions

The Activity

If children have trouble seeing that in the second bar 3/6 is equivalent to 1/2, you may want to separate the bar slightly along the middle into two groups of three tiles.

Although many children will not need the third clue to conclude that the solution is the second bar, the third clue provides them with verification of the solution.

Introducing

◆ Display these two fraction bars made from Color Tiles.

Y	R	R	B

B	B	Y	R	R	R

◆ Establish that each tile in the first bar represents one fourth and that each tile in the second bar represents one sixth.

◆ Ask volunteers to explain what fractional part each color represents in each fraction bar.

◆ Give the following set of fraction clues that describe one of the fraction bars. Stop after each clue and ask children which fraction bar is the solution and how they know.

The fraction bar is one-half red.
The fraction bar is one-third blue.
The fraction bar is one-sixth yellow.

On Their Own

Can you make a Color Tile fraction bar and then write a set of clues so that someone else could build it?

- Work with a partner. Choose 6, 8, 10, or 12 Color Tiles and arrange them in any way to form a fraction bar.

- Decide what fractional part of the whole bar is represented by each color you used. For example:

Blue: 2/6 or 1/3   Yellow: 1/6   Red: 3/6 or 1/2

- Record your fraction bar on grid paper. On the back of the paper, write a list of at least 3 clues that describe the fractional parts of your bar. Write each clue in this form:

  Our fraction bar is ——— blue.

- Exchange lists with another pair. Be careful not to peek at the back of the list! Follow the clues to try to build the other pair's fraction bar.

- When you have finished making the fraction bar, turn the list of clues over and compare what you built to the recording.

- Discuss your results with the other pair.

The Bigger Picture

Thinking and Sharing

Post children's drawings of their fraction bars. Lead children to talk about how they wrote clues for their own fraction bars and how they used other pair's clues to build fraction bars.

Use prompts such as these to promote class discussion:

- What clue did you write to describe the part of your own fraction bar that was blue? the part that was red? the green part? the yellow part?

- Did you need to read all the clues to build the other pair's fraction bar? Explain.

- If you could not build a matching fraction bar by following the other pair's clues, why do you think this happened?

- Is it possible for one set of clues to describe more than one fraction bar? Explain.

- Do you think that any of the clues you wrote should be changed? Why? How could you change them?

Writing

Have children make a fraction bar and write as many different fraction clues as they can about the colors in the bar.

Extending the Activity

1. Have two pairs work as a group to combine the tiles they used in their two fraction bars and then list five clues that describe this combined bar.

Where's the Mathematics?

Writing and solving riddles (sets of clues) about fractional parts of a whole fraction bar helps children gain a concrete understanding of the meaning of fractions, fractional equivalence, and how fractional parts relate to the whole. As children manipulate the Color Tiles, they have the opportunity to see, for example, why 2/8 red is the same as 1/4 red and how 1/5 + 2/10 + 3/5 equals one whole.

Children use their mathematics vocabulary as they describe their bar to one another in preparation for making up their clues. During their discussion, they have the opportunity to analyze their bars, noting things such as, "Three sixths of our fraction bar is red. That means half the bar is red." They can convince themselves of this by separating the red tiles from the nonred tiles and seeing that the two groups have the same number of tiles.

When trying to recreate the fraction bars from the clues, many children will use a trial-and-error approach—especially when the fractions in the clues have different denominators. This means they will try to build a 6-, 8-, 10-, and 12-tile bar to match the clues. If they have the chance to repeat the activity several times, some children may begin to search for a strategy. One such strategy might be to look at the largest denominator and try to express all the other fractions in terms of that denominator. If the denominator happens to be the same as the number of tiles in the bar, then the numerators indicate the number of each kind of tile.

Most children will produce a clue for each color in their fraction bars. However, if children use all four colors in making their fraction bars and limit their clues to three, it will be more of a challenge to recreate the fraction bar. In such cases, children may use addition and/or subtraction to identify the amount of the fourth color. Here is an example of a fraction bar and a set of clues that children might produce:

Our fraction bar is 1/4 red.
Our fraction bar is 3/8 green.
Our fraction bar is 1/8 yellow.

Children who are presented with the above clues would have to realize that the sum of 1/4 + 3/8 + 1/8 is less than 1. One way they could do this is to express all the fractions with the same denominator. Then they would be

Have them exchange lists with another group. Each group should follow the clues, using Color Tiles to try to build the combined fraction bar.

2. Challenge children to use 24 Color Tiles to make a fraction bar that is one-fourth blue, three-eighths green, one-eighth yellow, and one-fourth red.

3. Have pairs write two more clues, either for the fraction bar they made or for the one they tried to identify. Tell them to use the word *not* in both clues; for example, "This fraction bar is not one-fourth blue."

---

able to tell that there are two eighths that are not accounted for in the clues and that those two eighths must be blue.

Some children may be surprised to see that different numbers of tiles in different fraction bars can be represented by the same fraction. This gives them strong visual evidence that the size of the fraction depends on the size of the whole.

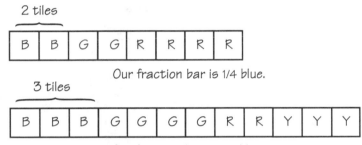

2 tiles

| B | B | G | G | R | R | R | R |

Our fraction bar is 1/4 blue.

3 tiles

| B | B | B | G | G | G | G | R | R | Y | Y | Y |

Our fraction bar is 1/4 blue.

Children may notice that, conversely, the same number of tiles may represent different fractions in different fraction bars.

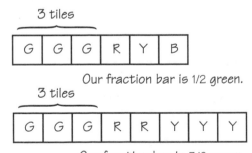

3 tiles

| G | G | G | R | Y | B |

Our fraction bar is 1/2 green.

3 tiles

| G | G | G | R | R | Y | Y | Y |

Our fraction bar is 3/8 green.

The same set of clues sometimes describes both a 6-tile fraction bar and a 12-tile fraction bar. This happens when the 12-tile bar has twice as many of each color tile as the 6-tile bar. For example:

Our fraction bar is 1/3 yellow.
Our fraction bar is 1/6 red.
Our fraction bar is 1/2 green.

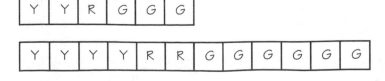

| Y | Y | R | G | G | G |

| Y | Y | Y | Y | R | R | G | G | G | G | G | G |

GROWING RECTANGLES

- • **Multiplication**
- • **Rectangles**
- • **Growth patterns**
- • **Predicting**

Getting Ready

What You'll Need

Color Tiles, 100 of each of 2 different colors per group

Color Tile grid paper, page 90 (optional)

Overhead Color Tiles and/or Color Tile grid paper transparency (optional)

Overview

Children use Color Tiles to build rectangles that "grow" in a predictable way. Then they predict the number of tiles needed to produce the rectangle that represents ten more stages of growth. In this activity, children have the opportunity to:

- ◆ search for patterns
- ◆ use patterns to make predictions
- ◆ use a rectangular array as a model for multiplication

The Activity

If children announce that the 2-by-2 rectangle looks like a square, you may want to point out that a square is, in fact, a rectangle with four equal sides.

Introducing

- ◆ Show children a 2-by-1 rectangle made from two Color Tiles of one color and have children copy it. Point out that this rectangle is 2 tiles long and 1 tile wide. Record its dimensions on the chalkboard as "2 x 1."

- ◆ Tell children to make their rectangle "grow" wider by adding tiles of a different color to change it into a 2-by-2 rectangle. Have a volunteer record the dimensions of this rectangle (2 x 2) below the dimensions of the first one.

- ◆ Direct children to add more tiles of the first color to make their rectangle grow wider again until it becomes a 2-by-3 rectangle. Ask a volunteer to record the dimensions of this rectangle (2 x 3).

- ◆ Have volunteers predict the dimensions of the next two larger rectangles and record them on the chalkboard. Then have children check their predictions of the growth patterns by building the two rectangles with these dimensions.

On Their Own

> **How can you use Color Tiles to make a rectangle "grow" longer and wider?**
>
> - Work with a group. Use 2 Color Tiles of the same color to make a rectangle that is 2 tiles long and 1 tile wide.
>
> - Use tiles of a different color to make your rectangle grow so that it is 1 tile longer and 1 tile wider than the starting rectangle.
>
> - Use the first color of tile to make the rectangle grow again so that it is 1 tile longer and 1 tile wider.
>
> - Record the first 3 stages of the rectangle's growth on grid paper.
>
> - Now make your rectangle grow 2 more times! Record these stages of growth.
>
> - Look for patterns in the number of Color Tiles used in each of the 5 stages of the rectangle's growth.
>
> - Suppose your rectangle grew 10 more times. Without building it, predict what it would look like and how many tiles it would have.
>
> - Be ready to tell how you were able to make your prediction.

The Bigger Picture

Thinking and Sharing

Ask children to suggest the best way to organize their data in order to see patterns emerge. You may wish to set up a table like this one and call on groups to contribute their data.

Size of Rectangle	Tiles in Rectangle	Tiles Added
2 x 1	2	—
3 x 2	6	4
4 x 3	12	6
5 x 4		

Some children may point out that by multiplying the dimensions of a rectangle, (l x w), they are applying the formula for finding the area of a rectangle. If children know how to apply the formula, allow them to do so instead of counting to find the number of "Tiles in Rectangle."

Use prompts such as these to promote class discussion:

- What did you notice as you built your rectangles?
- What patterns do you notice in the data?
- What is the same about the patterns? What is different?
- What did you do to predict the size of the rectangle if it grew ten more times?
- How could you find the data for the 100th row in the table?

Writing

Ask children to explain how the dimensions of a rectangle change as it grows. Have them include drawings of several stages of growth to illustrate their explanation.

Teacher Talk

Where's the Mathematics?

This activity gives children experience in exploring shapes to discover patterns and in predicting results based on those patterns. Children gain practice in organizing their data, thinking inductively, and using measurement vocabulary

By using contrasting colors to make their rectangles grow, children can see the pattern of tiles added.

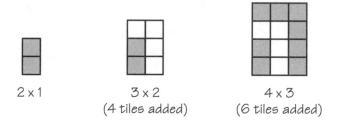

2 x 1	3 x 2	4 x 3
	(4 tiles added)	(6 tiles added)

The completed table should look like this.

Size of Rectangle	Tiles in Rectangle	Tiles Added
2 x 1	2	–
3 x 2	6	4
4 x 3	12	6
5 x 4	20	8
6 x 5	30	10
7 x 6	42	12
8 x 7	56	14
9 x 8	72	16
10 x 9	90	18
11 x 10	110	20
12 x 11	132	22
13 x 12	156	24
14 x 13	182	26
15 x 14	210	28
16 x 15	240	30

Extending the Activity

1. Challenge children to find the distance around, or perimeter of, each of the rectangles they built. Then ask them to tell what patterns they discovered by doing this.

2. Have children find the area of each of the rectangles they built in order, from smallest to largest. Then have them discuss how their solutions relate to the data in their tables.

By examining the data, some children may realize that by adding to both the length and the width of their rectangles with each new stage of growth, the following patterns emerge:

1. The numbers in the *Tiles in Rectangle* column are the products of the numbers in the *Size of Rectangle* column.

2. The numbers in the *Tiles in Rectangle* column are a sequence formed by adding successive even numbers beginning with 4.

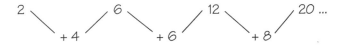

3. The numbers in the *Tiles Added* column form a sequence of even numbers beginning with 4. These numbers are also equal to two times the second dimensions (widths) of the rectangles.

Once children have an understanding of the patterns in their recordings and the table, they may be able to determine that the 100th rectangle will have the dimensions 101 x 100; will have 10,100 tiles; and will have 200 more tiles than the 99th rectangle.

Children should be encouraged to share their thinking and "shortcuts" with the class. If children complete one pattern of growing rectangles and record their data quickly, suggest that they begin again, this time with a rectangle of a different size, such as 2 by 4, then compare their data. Having a variety of results on the chalkboard may be of help to those children who have difficulty in seeing relationships within and across columns in a table.

LOGIC RIDDLES

Getting Ready

What You'll Need

Color Tiles, 10 each of red, yellow, blue, and green per pair

Small paper bags, 1 per pair

Paper clips, 1 per pair

Overview

Children create riddles that provide clues about Color Tiles that they have hidden in a paper bag. Then they try to solve one another's riddles. In this activity, children have the opportunity to:

- ◆ build logical reasoning skills
- ◆ make conjectures based on evidence
- ◆ find the fractional parts of a whole

The Activity

As you give each clue, you might want to write it on the chalkboard so that children can refer back to it during the discussion.

Introducing

- ◆ Display a sealed Riddle Bag containing four red, three yellow, two green, and three blue Color Tiles. Tell children that you will give clues to help them answer the riddle, "How many Color Tiles of each color are in this bag?"

- ◆ Give the first clue: *There are twelve tiles in my bag.* Have children follow this clue by counting out twelve tiles.

- ◆ Have children respond to the second clue: *The tiles are of four different colors.*

- ◆ Give the three following clues, pausing after each to allow children time to adjust their tiles to match it:
  Three-twelfths of the tiles in my bag are blue.
  There is one more red than blue.
  There is one more yellow than green.

- ◆ Have children display their solutions to the riddle. Then reveal the contents of the Riddle Bag.

- ◆ Discuss what qualities make a good riddle clue. Establish that each new clue should bring the solution closer.

- ◆ Point out that a good set of clues leads to just one solution.

On Their Own

Can you write a set of clues to make a Color Tile riddle?

- Work with a partner. Choose up to 12 Color Tiles.

- Count how many you have of each color. Discuss what fractional part each color represents.

- Decide on 3 or 4 good clues for a riddle that describes your tiles. Write them down. At least 1 of your clues must contain a fraction. Here is an example of a riddle for these Color Tiles.

R	R	R	R
Y	Y	Y	G
G	B	B	B

There are 12 tiles.
$3/12$ are blue.
There is 1 more red than blue.
There is 1 more yellow than green.

- Now test your riddle. Do this by pretending you don't know the answer and trying to solve it. If you can't solve the riddle, make changes to your clues so that the riddle has a solution.

- Put your tiles into the paper bag, close it, and clip your riddle to the bag.

- Exchange riddle bags with another pair. Try to solve their riddle. Then look into the bag to check your solution.

- Be prepared to talk about how you made and solved riddles.

The Bigger Picture

Thinking and Sharing

Invite children to talk about how they wrote and tested their own riddles and how they solved the riddles written by others.

Use prompts like these to promote class discussion:

- What words helped you to create clues?

- Did you ever change any tiles as you wrote your clues? Why?

- After reading the other pair's first clue, did you know anything for sure about the tiles in their bag? Explain.

- Did any clues tell about what was *not* in the bag? What were some of these?

- What kinds of clues give the most information?

- Does the order of the clues matter? Explain.

- If no one else can solve your riddle, what might be the reason?

- Was there more than one solution to any riddle? Why? Is there a way to change some clues to make that riddle have only one solution?

Tell children to imagine that Color Tiles come in two more sizes, 2-inch squares and 3-inch squares. Have them cut out cardboard squares of those

Teacher Talk

Where's the Mathematics?

The language of logic has been called the language of everyday life, since logical thinking underlies much of human activity. In this activity, children use language in a way that is mathematically powerful through words and phrases such as "All our tiles are blue or green," "Some of the tiles are yellow," "There are three more red than green," "None of the tiles are red," and "If there are seven tiles and two are red and there are no blues or greens, then five tiles must be yellow."

Children can easily write clues that identify their total number of tiles and the number of each color. They will have more difficulty writing clues that make comparisons within a group of tiles and those that identify fractional parts of the whole group. Initially, their clues need to be monitored closely for accuracy because children may have trouble wording their clues or may write too few clues.

Children will probably find solving riddles easier than writing them. Even though they may feel a certain comfort level in using their own words to communicate their ideas, children soon realize that they must take special care to see that their written clues really provide the information they are meant to convey. The task of writing clues helps children to become aware of the importance of using precise mathematical language.

When children create their clues, they are reasoning deductively as they use the number and color of the tiles to draw conclusions which are the written clues. When they solve the clues, they apply deductive reasoning again as they use the evidence of the written clues to come to a conclusion about the number and color of the tiles. As they gain more experience in dealing with clues, children may also gain an appreciation of the usefulness of clues that contain the words *not* or *no*. For example, if the bag has "no yellow tiles," children may conclude that the tiles in the bag are red, green, and/or blue.

As they write and test their riddles, children may discover and use different types of clues. Here are the clues written by three pairs of children. Notice the differences in the nature of the clues as well as which riddles are successful and which are not:

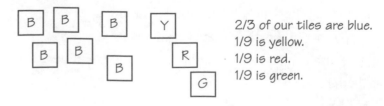

2/3 of our tiles are blue.
1/9 is yellow.
1/9 is red.
1/9 is green.

sizes and color them to match the Color Tiles. Allow them to use the tiles of three sizes as the basis of another riddle. After pairs solve each other's riddles, discuss how the tiles of the new sizes made a difference in writing and solving riddles.

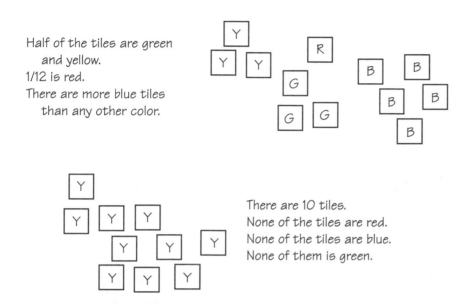

Half of the tiles are green and yellow.
1/12 is red.
There are more blue tiles than any other color.

There are 10 tiles.
None of the tiles are red.
None of the tiles are blue.
None of them is green.

You may want to present the second set of clues (the unsuccessful riddle) to children, challenging them to change the first clue or add a clue to make the riddle work.

Children may realize that the order in which the clues are presented or used can affect the difficulty of the riddle. Some children may first read all the clues and then try to satisfy the ones that seem most important, most difficult, or most useful. Consider this set of clues:

> *None of the tiles are blue or yellow.*
> *There is one more red than green.*
> *There are 7 tiles.*

Faced with these clues, children will find that it would be more challenging to use them in the order given than to scan them, then follow them in a *third-clue, first-clue, second-clue* order.

The skill of writing good riddles can be improved over time. Consider revisiting this activity periodically throughout the school year to provide children with the opportunity to master this skill.

LOOSE LINKS

Getting Ready

What You'll Need

Color Tiles, 35 per pair

Die, 1 per pair

Overhead Color Tiles and/or Color Tile grid paper transparency (optional)

Overview

Children play a game in which they start with a pile of 37 Color Tiles, then roll a die to determine the number of "chains" of equal length to make from the tiles. In this activity, children have the opportunity to:

◆ develop an understanding of division

◆ model the division algorithm

◆ find patterns in division facts

The Activity

You may want to explain that chains are made by "linking" Color Tiles, or lining them up in a row. Point out that any tiles that are left after equal chains are made are called "loose links."

You may want to play a game of Loose Links with children before they begin On Their Own.

Introducing

◆ Make a pile of 19 Color Tiles. Tell children that they will help you make these tiles into "chains" of equal length. On the chalkboard, write $\overline{)19}$.

◆ Have a volunteer roll a die. Explain that the number rolled tells how many chains of equal length to make from the 19 tiles. Make that number of chains and set aside the leftover tiles, or "loose link(s)." For example, if 5 is rolled, make 5 chains of 3 tiles each and set aside the 4 remaining tiles.

◆ Explain that for each roll of the die, there is a way to record the number of chains that can be made and any loose link(s) that remain. Then, complete the division on the chalkboard. For the example above, write the following: $5\overline{)19}\,^{3}\,R4$

◆ Now, point out that you will set aside the 4 loose links and use the Color Tiles that remain to write a new division problem, $\overline{)15}$. Have another volunteer roll the die and repeat the activity.

On Their Own

Play *Loose Links!*

Here are the rules:

1. This is a game for 2 players. The object is to be the player who has the greater number of Color Tiles when the game ends.

2. Players make a pile of 37 Color Tiles. They decide who will go first.

3. The first player writes the beginning of a division problem, $\overline{37}$, and rolls the die to find out how many chains of equal length to make from the 37 tiles.

4. The first player makes chains that are as long as possible, and says how many "loose link" tiles are left, then completes the division problem. For example, if a 5 was rolled:

$$7 \leftarrow \text{Number of tiles in each chain}$$
$$\text{Number of chains} \rightarrow 5\overline{)37} \; \text{R2} \leftarrow \text{Number of loose link tiles}$$

5. Now, the first player takes and keeps any loose links.

6. The second player begins a turn using the tiles that are left. Since there were 2 loose links in the example above, the second player would begin with 35 tiles and would write $\overline{35}$.

7. Players keep playing until all the Color Tiles have been taken. Whoever ends up with more tiles wins the game.

- Play at least 2 full games of *Loose Links*.

- Look for patterns in the division problems.

The Bigger Picture

Thinking and Sharing

Write these headings across the chalkboard: *0 Loose Links, 1 Loose Link, 2 Loose Links, 3 Loose Links, 4 Loose Links,* and *5 Loose Links*. Have children post their division problems in the appropriate columns according to their remainders, or loose links.

Use prompts like these to promote class discussion:

- What patterns did you notice in the division problems?

- For which numbers could you make two chains with no loose links? For which could you make three chains with no loose links? How about four chains? five? six?

- What happened when a 1 was rolled?

- Which numbers always had loose links unless a 1 was rolled?

- Which numbers had the greatest number of ways to get chains with no loose links? What happened in the game when these numbers were rolled?

Writing

Ask children to tell how they knew what division problem to write at the beginning of one of their turns.

<table>
<tr><td>**Teacher Talk**</td></tr>
</table>

Where's the Mathematics?

This activity provides an introduction to the concept of division as the partitioning of a set into equal-sized groups. It also conveys the meaning of "remainder." Multiplication facts are reinforced when children start rounds of play having to determine how many Snap Cubes are left so they can begin their division problem.

Children are likely to note that 1 is a divisor of every number; in other words, dividing by 1 always leaves a remainder of zero. Children are also likely to point out that the remainder (the number of tiles or loose links) is always less than the divisor (the number of chains). Children can verify this by examining the chains and the number of loose links. If the number of loose links is equal to or greater than the number of chains, then each of the chains can be made longer.

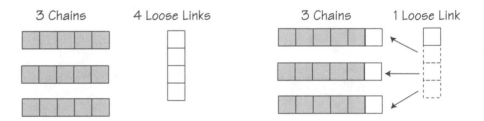

Children will notice that each of the numbers 2, 4, 6, 8, 10, 12, 14, 16, 18, 20, 22, 24, 26, 28, 30, 32, 34, and 36 can be made into two chains of equal length with no remainders. They will recognize these numbers as even numbers and perhaps supply their own definition of even numbers as "the doubles" or "numbers that make equal chains with no leftovers when you roll a 2."

When children look at the numbers that have 3 as a divisor and no remainder—namely, 3, 6, 9, 12, 15, 18, 21, 24, 27, 30, 33, and 36—they will be reminded of the multiplication table for 3. They may notice that this

Extending the Activity

1. Have children play *Loose Links* again, this time using a number cube marked with the numbers 2, 4, 6, 8, 10, and 12 instead of a die.

2. Have children play the game again, but this time, have them begin either with more than or fewer than 37 Color Tiles.

list includes every third number from the list of even numbers and has an odd-even pattern.

Four is a divisor for 4, 8, 12, 16, 20, 24, 28, 32, and 36. These numbers are made up of every other number from the even list. As the size of the divisor increases, the list of numbers shortens. By the time children get to the numbers that have 5 as a divisor, there are only seven: 5, 10, 15, 20, 25, 30 and 35. The list for 6 is even shorter with only six numbers: 6, 12, 18, 24, 30, and 36.

Children are apt to report that 12, 24, and 36 are the numbers they got "stuck on" in the game. By this, they mean that any roll of the die, except 5, resulted in chains with an equal number of tiles and no leftover tiles; so play went back and forth between the two players with no one winning any loose links until a 5 was rolled.

When the children look for numbers that always give loose links (unless a 1 was rolled), they will find 7, 11, 13, 17, 19, 23, 29, 31, and 37. Later, children will learn that these numbers are part of the set called *prime numbers*, which have exactly two divisors: the number itself and 1. The prime numbers 2, 3, and 5 would not belong on the children's list because these numbers have no leftovers when the numbers themselves (2, 3, or 5) are rolled.

By a lucky roll of the die or if the children have played the game enough to be able to compile exhaustive lists of data, they will see that the numbers 11, 17, 23, 29, and 35 hold the potential for rolling a 6 on the die and netting the greatest number of loose links possible for this game (5).

In analyzing the parts of their division problems—namely, the dividend, divisor, quotient, and remainder—children get their first taste of the study of number theory and a foundation for dealing with division in an algebraic context.

PATTERNS OF SYMMETRY

- **Symmetry**
- **Congruence**
- **Spatial visualization**

Getting Ready

What You'll Need

Color Tiles, 200, 50 of each color per group

6 x 6 Color Tile grids, 4 per group, page 95

Crayons

Mirrors (optional)

Overhead Color Tiles and/or Color Tile grid paper transparency (optional)

Overview

Children use Color Tiles to create square designs with various lines of symmetry. Then they try to identify symmetry in one another's designs. In this activity, children have the opportunity to:

- ◆ create a design that has line symmetry

- ◆ analyze a design to determine whether or not it has line symmetry

The Activity

You may want to demonstrate how to use a mirror to check for symmetry by holding it along a possible line of symmetry. Point out that if the reflection children see in the mirror shows the matching part of the design (the part on the other side of the mirror), then they can be sure that they have found a line of symmetry.

Introducing

- ◆ Display this Color Tile design. Have children copy, then record it.

- ◆ Show children how to fold their recordings so that the fold line divides the design into two parts that cover each other exactly.

- ◆ Ask volunteers to compare the two parts made by the fold line. Confirm that one part is like a reflection of the other in a mirror.

- ◆ Explain that when a design can be folded upon itself in this way, mathematicians say that the design has *symmetry* and the fold line is called the *line of symmetry*.

- ◆ Point out that some designs have more than one line of symmetry. Make sure children understand why this design has both horizontal and vertical lines of symmetry.

On Their Own

Can you use Color Tiles to make designs that have lines of symmetry?

- With a group, work on 6-by-6 grids that look like this:

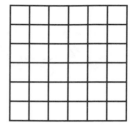

- Use 2 or more colors of tiles to make a design that completely covers the grid and has a line of symmetry.

- Here's how to decide if a design has line symmetry: Imagine a line drawn through the middle of your design. If you could fold the design along that line so that 1 part of the design fit exactly on top of the other and all the colors matched, the design would have line symmetry. These figures show the 4 possible lines of symmetry for a square design.

- Make 4 designs, 1 to fit each rule:
  - Design A must have only 1 line of symmetry.
  - Design B must have only 2 lines of symmetry.
  - Design C must have 4 lines of symmetry.
  - Design D must have *no* lines of symmetry.

- Check your designs for line symmetry by holding a mirror along what you think is the line of symmetry. If you see the matching half of the design reflected in the mirror, then the line is a line of symmetry.

- Record your designs on the grids. Label each A, B, C, or D.

- Be ready to tell how you went about making each design.

The Bigger Picture

Thinking and Sharing

Write the column headings *A, B, C,* and *D* across the chalkboard. Call on groups to post their designs under the appropriate headings. Give the class an opportunity to check and adjust the postings.

Use prompts like these to promote class discussion:

- How can you tell if a design has line symmetry?
- Look at any column. How is the symmetry in the designs alike? How does it differ?
- How can you check that a design has no symmetry?
- When is it easy to see a line of symmetry in a design? When is it hard?

Drawing and Writing

Have children advise someone else how to use Color Tiles to make a symmetrical design. Ask them to make descriptive drawings to accompany their writing.

Extending the Activity

Challenge children to make Color Tile designs that have line symmetry but do not completely cover the 6-by-6 grid.

Where's the Mathematics?

This activity will heighten children's awareness of symmetry. Symmetrical design elements in clothing, wallpaper, and buildings lend a kind of comfort, or consistency, that is pleasing to the eye.

Here are possible Color Tile designs that children might produce having one, two, four, or no lines of symmetry. Most children will be able to produce designs with horizontal and vertical lines of symmetry. Some will have difficulty with diagonal lines of symmetry because the lines "cut" through squares in the design.

A—1 Line of Symmetry

Y	Y	Y	Y	Y	Y
Y	Y	Y	Y	Y	Y
B	Y	Y	Y	Y	B
Y	B	Y	Y	B	Y
Y	Y	B	B	Y	Y
Y	Y	Y	Y	Y	Y

Y	Y	Y	Y	Y	Y
Y	Y	Y	Y	Y	Y
Y	Y	B	B	Y	Y
Y	Y	B	B	Y	Y
B	B	Y	Y	B	B
B	B	Y	Y	B	B

Y	Y	Y	B	B	B
Y	Y	Y	B	B	B
B	B	B	B	B	B
B	B	B	B	B	B
Y	Y	Y	B	B	B
Y	Y	Y	B	B	B

B—Exactly 2 Lines of Symmetry

R	G	R	R	G	R
R	G	R	R	G	R
R	G	R	R	G	R
R	G	R	R	G	R
R	G	R	R	G	R
R	G	R	R	G	R

R	R	R	R	R	R
R	R	R	R	R	R
G	G	G	G	G	G
G	G	G	G	G	G
R	R	R	R	R	R
R	R	R	R	R	R

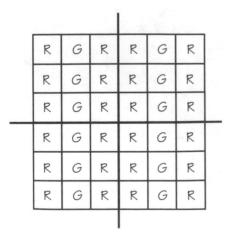

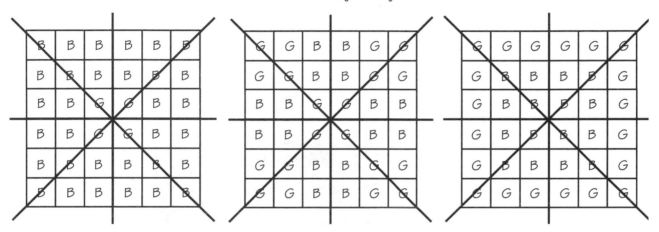

C—4 Lines of Symmetry

D—No Lines of Symmetry (Asymmetry)

Children's strategies will vary. Some will use a trial-and-error approach—creating a design, checking with the mirror, and making adjustments. Others may develop a systematic approach. One such system would be to draw the desired line of symmetry on the outline and then place tiles of the same colors on corresponding squares on each side of the line.

Reflection is key to the idea of symmetry. Children may realize that both parts of the design must be congruent in terms of shape and color, but they may confuse congruent parts that show a translation (or slide) and congruent parts that show a reflection. The first design at the right shows a translation (or slide) of the figure across the line that is not a line of symmetry. The second shows a reflection of the figure across the line that is a line of symmetry.

Translation   Reflection

PENTOMINOES

GEOMETRY • PATTERNS/FUNCTIONS • LOGIC

- • Spatial visualization
- • Congruence
- • Transformational geometry
- • Sorting

Getting Ready

What You'll Need

Color Tiles, 5 of 1 color per child

Color Tile grid paper, several sheets per pair, page 90

Crayons

Envelopes, 1 per pair

Overhead Color Tiles and/or Color Tile grid paper transparency (optional)

Overview

Children manipulate five Color Tiles in order to discover all the possible arrangements, or *pentominoes,* that can be made. In this activity, children have the opportunity to:

- ◆ devise strategies for finding and sorting shapes
- ◆ reinforce their understanding of congruence by flipping and turning figures in order to compare them

The Activity

You may wish to point out that the following arrangement of four squares is not a tetramino because a full side of one tile is touching only part of the sides of two other tiles.

Introducing

- ◆ Display a row of four Color Tiles of one color.
- ◆ Point out that any shape made up of four squares, with at least one full side of each square touching a full side of another square, is called a *tetramino.*
- ◆ Ask children to use Color Tiles to copy your tetramino. Then challenge them to build as many different tetraminoes as they can.
- ◆ Call on several volunteers to display their tetraminoes near yours.
- ◆ Ask children whether any of the arrangements displayed have exactly the same shape. Have them explain their responses.
- ◆ If two or more tetraminoes appear to be different but are, in fact, congruent, point out how one of them can be flipped and/or turned to look exactly the same as the other. Establish that if such tetraminoes are congruent, they are not considered to be different from one another.

© ETA/Cuisenaire®

On Their Own

Can you find all the possible pentominoes using Color Tiles?

- With a partner, use 5 Color Tiles of 1 color to make a pentomino. A *pentomino* is a shape made of 5 squares, each of which has at least 1 full side touching 1 full side of another square.

Pentominoes   Not Pentominoes

- Record your pentomino. Then make a different pentomino.

- Keep on making and recording pentominoes until you cannot make any more that are different.

- Cut out your pentominoes. Compare them by flipping and turning them to see if any match exactly. If you find a match, keep only 1 of them.

- Number your pentominoes and put them in an envelope. Write your names and the number of pentominoes on the envelope.

- Exchange envelopes with another pair. Check their pentominoes to see if any of them are the same. Mark any that you think are exactly the same.

- Return the envelopes. Check your envelope to see if any duplicates were found.

- Talk about ways you could sort your pentominoes.

The Bigger Picture

Thinking and Sharing

Ask one or two pairs of children to post their pentominoes in an organized way. Note the organizations, then discuss each of the posted pentominoes. Point out any duplicates and figures that are not pentominoes. Call on volunteers to supply any missing pentominoes.

Use prompts like these to promote class discussion:

- Do you think that you have found all possible pentominoes? Explain.

- In what ways do the arrangements differ from one another?

- What strategies did you use to make new pentominoes from your old ones?

- Did you find any patterns while making your pentominoes? Did you use these patterns when sorting them? How?

- Did sorting your pentominoes help you find others that were missing? If so, explain.

Drawing and Writing

Have children make a poster pairing each of the twelve unique pentominoes with a flip or turn (rotation) of it. Ask them to explain their work by telling how the members of each pair are related.

Extending the Activity

Have children examine their pentominoes and predict which of them could be folded along the grid lines to form an open box. Then have children fold these pentominoes along the grid lines to check their predictions.

Teacher Talk

Children might find it of interest to know that penta *is the Greek root meaning "five" and* ominoes *refers to the squares that make up the whole figure.*

Where's the Mathematics?

Children may use many different strategies in their search for the twelve possible pentominoes. Some will create shapes by moving the five Color Tiles around at random, each time completely destroying the previously made pentomino before beginning on the next. Others may start by placing their five tiles in a row and moving one tile along the length of the remaining four to see how many unique pentominoes they can find.

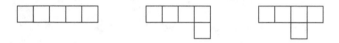

Children may then work with three tiles in a row, examining possible locations for the remaining two tiles.

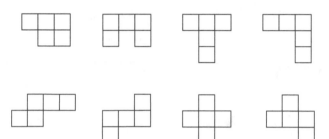

Finally, children may find the remaining pentomino by creating a staircase-like arrangement of the five tiles.

Children will have different ways of sorting their pentominoes. Some will sort them in the order in which they discovered them, perhaps beginning with the longest number of tiles in a row as outlined above. Others may sort them according to those that appear to be "block shapes" and those that are "not block shapes."

Still others may organize their pentominoes according to the letters of the alphabet that they resemble.

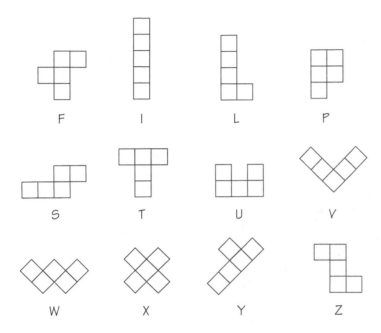

When they check to see that they have found all the possible pentominoes, some children may discover that they have inadvertently made duplicate shapes. For example, note the two orientations of one pentomino that one pair of children identified as two different pentominoes:

Any children confronted with two of the same pentominoes should be helped to recognize that the two are congruent. This can be done by allowing children to handle two cutouts of the pentomino in question and encouraging them to turn and flip the two to see how one fits exactly over the other.

SIDES AND ANGLES

- Counting
- Comparing
- Polygons
- Organizing data
- Interpreting data

Getting Ready

What You'll Need

Color Tiles, 50 per pair

Color Tile grid paper, several sheets per pair, page 90

Crayons

Overhead Color Tiles and/or Color Tile grid paper transparency (optional)

Overview

Children try to build as many arrangements of eight Color Tiles as they can. Then they determine which arrangements have the fewest and the greatest numbers of sides and angles. In this activity, children have the opportunity to:

- ◆ record and interpret data

- ◆ explore the relationship between the number of sides and the number of angles of a polygon

The Activity

You may wish to advise children who have difficulty counting the sides of the last shape to move a finger along its perimeter while keeping track of their starting point so as not to retrace it.

Recording a shape, then shading it, may keep children from making the mistake of counting the corners of individual tiles instead of the corners of the whole shape.

Introducing

- ◆ Make and display these three Color Tile arrangements.

- ◆ Ask volunteers to tell how these shapes are alike.

- ◆ After eliciting the likenesses, ask children to tell how the shapes differ. Elicit that the last shape has a different number of sides than the others.

- ◆ Now ask children to find the number of corners, or angles, in each shape.

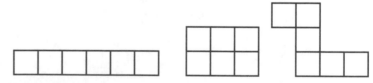

- ◆ Establish that shapes made up of the same number of tiles can have different numbers of sides and angles.

On Their Own

How many 8-tile shapes can you make that have different numbers of sides and angles?

- With a partner, make a shape using 8 Color Tiles. Your shape must follow this rule:

  *Every tile must share at least
  1 full side with another tile.*   *There can be no "holes" in a shape.*

  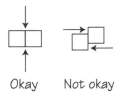

  Okay   Not okay   Not okay

- Use more tiles to make as many different 8-tile shapes as you can that follow the same rule.

- Record your shapes on grid paper. Then cut them out.

- Check your shapes to be sure they are all different. (Remember, if a shape can be covered exactly by a flip or turn of another shape, the 2 shapes are really the same!)

- Put your shapes facedown so that you can't see the grid marks.

- Now, looking at the back of each shape, find the number of sides and the number of angles. Write the numbers on the back.

- Decide on a way to sort your shapes. Be ready to talk about what you notice

The Bigger Picture

Thinking and Sharing

Invite a pair to post their shape with the least number of sides and angles. Call for other pairs to post shapes that look different but have the same number of sides and angles. Label the number of sides and angles for this group of postings. Now invite a pair to post their shape with the greatest number of sides and angles. Have others post shapes that look different but have the same number of sides and angles. Label the number of sides and angles for these postings.

Use prompts like these to promote class discussion:

- How did you go about making your different shapes?

- What different numbers of sides and angles did you find for your shapes?

- What did you notice about the sides and angles in each of your shapes?

- Why do you think that four is the least number of sides and angles that can be made with eight Color Tiles? Why do you think that sixteen is the greatest number?

Extending the Activity

Have children work in groups to find the fewest and greatest numbers of sides and angles that can be made from shapes having from one to seven Color Tiles. Have them record their findings, then review them. Ask children

Where's the Mathematics?

Through their investigation, most children will begin to realize that each shape they build has an equal number of sides and angles. Children may be surprised to learn that this is true not only for the 8-tile shapes they work with in this activity but also for shapes made from other numbers of Color Tiles. If they have already done the activity *Ben's Garden Plot,* you may want to have them verify this fact by counting the numbers of sides and angles in each of the 10-tile designs they made for it.

In order to make their different arrangements of eight Color Tiles, children will take various approaches. Many may begin with a single row of eight, then go on to reposition one or more tiles in different ways to create more complex shapes. Others may begin by making the more complex shapes first, then work toward making the simpler ones. Still others will use a random approach. Whichever they choose, recording then sorting their shapes gives children an opportunity to analyze each to see how it fits into the scheme.

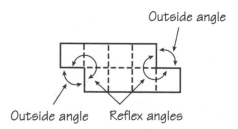

Outside angle

Outside angle   Reflex angles

Most children will have no difficulty counting the interior right angles in each shape. However, the other kinds of interior angles that show up in these shapes are reflex angles that measure 270 degrees, and these may be hard for children to recognize as angles. In fact, when they count the angles in a shape and come to the reflex angles, they may instead count the right angles they see outside the shape that share vertices with the interior reflex angles. If children do this, they will still get the correct totals for the number of angles, but at some point you may wish to visit the concept of reflex angles.

Using eight tiles, it is possible to build shapes having these numbers of sides and angles: 4, 8, 10, 12, 14, and 16. Children's shapes will look like some of these:

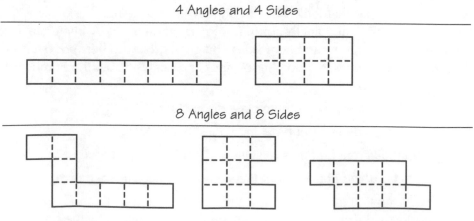

4 Angles and 4 Sides

8 Angles and 8 Sides

if they can predict the fewest and greatest numbers of sides and angles for a shape made from nine tiles. Record their predictions, then have them build the shapes to verify their predictions.

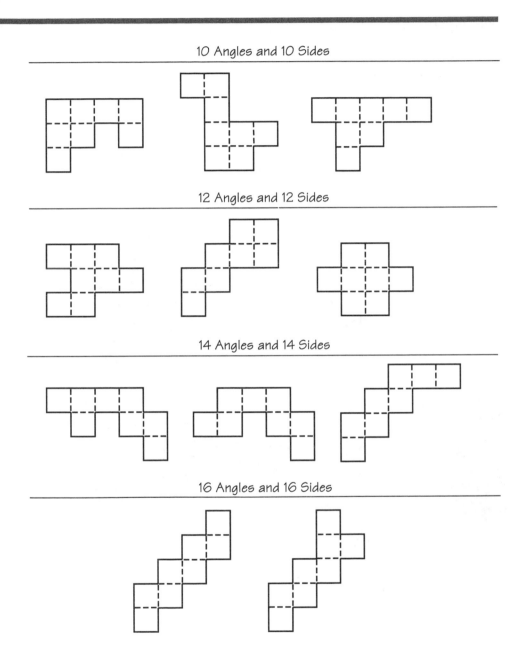

10 Angles and 10 Sides

12 Angles and 12 Sides

14 Angles and 14 Sides

16 Angles and 16 Sides

It may be difficult for children to explain why four is the fewest number of sides and angles that a shape made from eight tiles can have and why 16 is the greatest. You may want to help them by pointing out that four is also the fewest number of sides and angles that a shape made from six tiles can have, but, in this case, 12 is the greatest. Similarly, four is the fewest number for a 9-tile shape, while 18 is the greatest.

SQUARES IN A SQUARE

- Number sequences
- Spatial visualization
- Patterns

Getting Ready

What You'll Need

Color Tiles, 36 of 1 color per group

6-by-6 Color Tile grid, several per group, page 95, or Color Tile grid paper, page 90

Tracing paper, several sheets per group

Crayons

Overhead Color Tiles and/or Color Tile grid paper transparency (optional)

Overview

Children use Color Tiles to learn about square numbers as they try to find all the squares contained in a 6-by-6 square figure. In this activity, children have the opportunity to:

- ◆ develop counting techniques
- ◆ collect and analyze data
- ◆ discover number patterns and use them to make predictions

The Activity

Some children may need to record the figure, then use crayons of different colors to outline each square they see.

Introducing

- ◆ Display a 2-by-2 square figure made from four Color Tiles of one color and have children copy it.
- ◆ Ask a pair of children to find the number of squares in this figure.
- ◆ Elicit that the 2-by-2 figure contains four 1-by-1 squares and one 2-by-2 square for a total of five squares.
- ◆ Then have children find the number of squares in a 3-by-3 Color Tile figure.
- ◆ Establish that, in the 3-by-3 figure, there are nine one-by-one squares, four 2-by-2 squares, and one 3-by-3 square.

On Their Own

How many squares can you find in a 6-by-6 square figure made of Color Tiles?

- Work with a group. Use 1 color of Color Tiles to build a square with 6 tiles on a side.

- Talk about how to find and count all the different squares that are in this square. Squares that are the same size are counted separately if they are in different parts of the 6-by-6 square. For example, you would count these 3-by-3 squares separately.

- Find and record the number of different squares of each size (1-by-1 through 6-by-6) that are in the 6-by-6 square.

- Be ready to explain how you found the number of squares of each size and the number of squares in the whole 6-by-6 square figure.

The Bigger Picture

Thinking and Sharing

Have volunteers share their groups' methods of finding squares of each size and their ways of recording their findings. Compile findings in a chart like this:

Size of Square	6 by 6	5 by 5	4 by 4	3 by 3	2 by 2	1 by 1
Number of Squares						

Use prompts like these to promote class discussion:

- How big is the smallest square you found? How big is the largest?

- What is the size of another square in this figure? How did you go about finding all the squares of that size?

- Did your way of recording make it easy to keep track of your findings? Do you think that another way of recording might have worked better? Why?

- What patterns did you find in the numbers of squares of each size?

- How many squares are there in the figure?

Writing

Have children explain which size square was the most difficult to keep track of and why.

Extending the Activity

Display a checkerboard. Challenge children to find the number of squares on the checkerboard. You may want to get them started by pointing out that they have already done much of the work of solving this problem.

Where's the Mathematics?

Identifying the overlapping squares of various sizes is a challenging task. Children may find it helpful to tape a piece of tracing paper over a 6 x 6 grid to first trace around all the 5 x 5 squares. They can then use new sheets of tracing paper to trace around each of the 4 x 4 squares, the 3 x 3 squares, and the 2 x 2 squares.

Children can readily see that the 6-by-6 figure itself forms one square and that there are 36 of the 1-by-1 squares. Whereas some groups will try to determine the number of smaller squares of each size contained in the 6-by-6 figure, others may take the approach of trying to rebuild the figure several times over, each time rebuilding it from different squares of a smaller size and keeping track of the number of smaller squares as they build. Some groups may work in order, either beginning with the smallest squares and working up to the largest or beginning with the largest square and working down to the smallest. Others may work in random order. Whichever way they work, what is crucial is that they record their results, examine the data, and develop their ability to discover number patterns.

A group that chooses to collect its data by outlining squares of a given size may start with figures like these in which the given square is placed in the upper left corner. Then by shifting the square and outlining its new position each time, they find the total number for that size square. For example, the 5-by-5 square can be traced in its starting position. Then it can be shifted once to the right and outlined, once down and outlined, and once to the left and outlined, making a total of four squares.

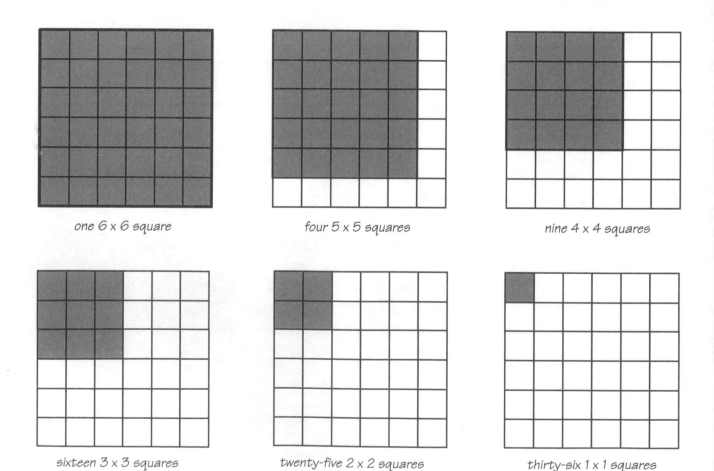

one 6 x 6 square   four 5 x 5 squares   nine 4 x 4 squares

sixteen 3 x 3 squares   twenty-five 2 x 2 squares   thirty-six 1 x 1 squares

The data thus collected can then be recorded in the chart.

Size of Square	6 by 6	5 by 5	4 by 4	3 by 3	2 by 2	1 by 1
Number of Squares	1	4	9	16	25	36

With the completion of the chart, some children may think that they have solved the problem. They need to be reminded that in order to find the number of squares contained in the 6-by-6 figure, they must find the sum of 1, 4, 9, 16, 25, and 36, or 91.

In highlighting the number of squares of each size, children are introduced to the beginning of the sequence of *square numbers*. Greek mathematicians gave the sequence this name because only such numbers be represented with square arrays. For example, the first six square numbers can be represented as follows:

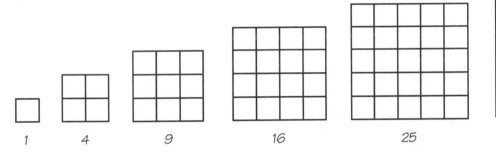

1   4   9   16   25   36

Once children chart their data, they may notice emerging patterns. They may, for instance, discover the pattern that can be used to predict the number of different squares in larger squares: *The number of different squares in a square of a certain size is equal to the sum of the number of tiles it took to build that square plus the number of different squares in the square of the next smaller size.* This becomes apparent in the following table:

Number of Units in Side of Square	Number of Color Tiles in Square	Total Number of Squares
1	1	1
2	4	5 (1 +4)
3	9	14 (5 + 9)
4	16	30 (14 + 16)
5	25	55 (30 + 25)
6	36	91 (55 + 36)

Children may also notice that the differences between 1 and 4, 4 and 9, and 9 and 16 are the odd numbers, 3, 5, and 7, respectively. Investigating the pattern further, children can conclude that consecutive square numbers always differ by an odd number. The ability to discover such number patterns is an extremely useful skill enabling children to solve problems, formulate conjectures, and draw generalizations.

TAKE YOUR PICK

Getting Ready

What You'll Need

Paper bags (each containing 10 Color Tiles, 3 green, 7 yellow), 1 per group

Paper bag containing 5 Color Tiles, 1 red and 4 blue

Overview

Children pick a Color Tile from a bag, then replace it. They repeat the process until they think they can predict the colors of the tiles in the bag based on the results of their picks. In this activity, children have the opportunity to:

◆ experience sampling with replacement

◆ investigate probability

◆ collect and organize data

The Activity

You may want to explain that when you predict something you make a guess based on information.

Introducing

◆ Hold up the bag of five Color Tiles and tell children that there are five tiles in this bag—some red and some blue. Explain that without looking into the bag, they will gather information to predict the number of tiles of each color.

◆ Ask a volunteer to pick a tile from the bag without looking, record its color on the chalkboard, then return it to the bag.

◆ Have other volunteers repeat the process, shaking the bag to mix up the tiles before each new pick.

◆ After a few picks, ask several volunteers to predict the number of each color of tile in the bag, explain their predictions, then record these predictions on the chalkboard.

◆ Spill the tiles from the bag, allowing children to compare their predictions to the actual contents.

On Their Own

Can you predict how many tiles there are of each of 2 colors in a bag that contains 10 Color Tiles?

- Work with a group. Take a bag of Color Tiles. The bag contains a total of 10 Color Tiles—some yellow and some green. Don't peek inside.

- Take turns doing the following:

  - Pick a tile from the bag without looking.

  - Record the color of the tile.

  - Return the tile to the bag and shake the bag so that the tiles are mixed for the next person's turn.

- Continue taking turns and repeating the process until you agree that you have enough information to predict the number of yellow and green tiles in the bag.

- Make a prediction and write it down.

- Spill the tiles from the bag. Compare the contents to what you predicted.

- Be ready to explain how you made your prediction.

The Bigger Picture

Thinking and Sharing

Encourage the groups to share what they did—how many times they picked, how they kept track of their picks, and their reasons for making their predictions. Lead them to note any relationships between the number of picks a group made and how well they predicted. Collect results from various groups in charts that look like the one below. Then work with children to create a chart showing the combined results for the entire class.

Yellow	~~HHHT~~ ~~HHHT~~ ||
Green	~~HHHT~~ |||

Use prompts such as these to promote class discussion:

- How many picks did you make before you predicted?
- Did everyone in your group agree on when it was time to predict? Explain.
- How close was your prediction to what was actually in the bag?
- Suppose your group took ten more picks before predicting. Do you think your prediction might have been different? Why?
- How does the data in the class chart reflect the contents of the bag?

Writing

Have children explain what they could have done to be even more sure of predicting correctly.

Extending the Activity

1. Make up bags of ten Color Tiles containing tiles of any combination of three colors. Have groups repeat the activity using these bags. Help them to compare these results with their results in the original activity. Lead

Where's the Mathematics?

In this activity, since children are picking Color Tiles from a bag without looking, each tile has an equally likely chance of being picked. Also, since each tile picked is then returned to the bag, the fact that it has been picked previously has no effect on whether or not it will be picked again.

Knowing that there are two colors of tiles in the bag of ten may predispose some children into thinking that there are five tiles of each color. (Such a misconception might be corrected by reminding children of the results of the *Introducing* activity in which, out of five tiles, four were of one color and only one was of another color.) Other children might approach the activity by listing the possible combinations of the two colors of ten tiles, realizing that one of them will reflect the actual contents of the bag:

1 yellow and 9 green	1 green and 9 yellow
2 yellow and 8 green	2 green and 8 yellow
3 yellow and 7 green	3 green and 7 yellow
4 yellow and 6 green	4 green and 6 yellow
5 yellow and 5 green	

Each time children pick a tile, they are taking a sample. The process of picking, then replacing, a tile is called *sampling and replacing*.

Sharing the various ways groups keep track of their sampling increases children's awareness that data may be recorded in different ways, each of which may be legitimate as long as it presents the data so that it can be easily read and interpreted. Some groups will start off the activity by preparing a chart for the collection of their data. Others will not address children to discuss whether or not the addition of a third color of tile made a difference.

2. Put 100 Color Tiles of any combinations of four colors into a bag. Have children take turns picking 10 tiles at a time, recording the colors, then returning the tiles to the bag. After several picks, tell children to begin picking 20 tiles at a time, then continue the procedure. Have children decide when to make a prediction, advising them to think about what they can do to increase the likelihood of making a good prediction.

the issue of how and where to record their data until the first tile has been picked.

Children use different strategies for deciding when they have enough data to make a prediction. Some may give each group member one or two picks and decide that that number of picks is sufficient. Some may decide that since there are ten tiles in the bag, ten picks is sufficient. Children who surmise that more picks may lead to a better prediction will make more than ten picks and then apply some kind of proportional reasoning to the data. For example, if a group makes twenty picks with 13 yellows and 7 greens, they may decide simply that there are more yellows than greens and choose one of the following as the contents of the bag: 9 yellows and 1 green, 8 yellows and 2 greens, 7 yellows and 3 greens, or 6 yellows and 4 greens. Children who can do proportional reasoning would realize that 13 is about twice 6 and so predict that there are 7 yellows and 3 greens, since 7 is about twice 3.

Point out to children that although proportional reasoning is a good tool for making predictions based on a sample, it will not guarantee an accurate prediction. For example, if in twenty picks there are 11 yellows and 9 greens, a reasonable prediction would be 5 yellows and 5 greens or 6 yellows and 4 greens—predictions that reflect a sample that does not accurately reflect the contents of the bag.

Some children may be lucky and come up with an accurate prediction with a minimal amount of data. These children may initially be convinced that they have found a system that always works. However, once the class comes together and compares and compiles its data, most children will see that more picks usually lead to more accurate predictions.

TILE LOGIC PUZZLES

- • Comparing
- • Transformational geometry
- • Spatial visualization

Getting Ready

What You'll Need

Color Tiles, 4 of each color per pair

4 x 4 Color Tile grids, several per pair, page 92, or Color Tile grid paper, page 90

Crayons

Overhead Color Tiles and/or Color Tile grid paper transparency (optional)

Overview

Children arrange Color Tiles to form a square formation according to a given set of rules. In this activity, children have the opportunity to:

- ◆ use logical reasoning
- ◆ develop a design that satisfies specific conditions
- ◆ discover a new solution based on an old one

Puzzle Rules
1. No two tiles of the same color can touch.
   - horizontally
   - vertically
   - diagonally
2. No two rows can have the same sequence of colors.

The Activity

You may want to distribute 3-by-3 grids cut from 1-inch grid paper for children's use as a guide for positioning their tiles.

Introducing

- ◆ Display this formation of Color Tiles. Have pairs of children copy it.

- ◆ Ask children how many more tiles they would need to add to the formation to make it a square with three tiles on each side.

- ◆ Direct children to find the correct color of tiles to make the 3-by-3 square according to these rules:

  1. The completed square must have 3 blue tiles, 3 red tiles, and 3 yellow tiles.

  2. No two tiles of the same color may touch along their sides—either across or up and down.

- ◆ When children have found the solution, invite them to tell how they decided where to position the tiles of each color.

B		R
	B	Y
R	B	

B	Y	R
R	B	Y
Y	R	B

On Their Own

Can you follow a set of rules to form a square arrangement of Color Tiles?

- Work with a partner. Use 16 Color Tiles to form a square according to these rules:
  - The square must have 4 of each color of tile.
  - No 2 tiles of the same color may touch along a side.
  - No 2 tiles of the same color may touch at a corner.
  - The order of the colors in each row must differ from the order in every other row.

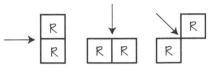

Not okay   Not okay   Not okay

- Record your square.

- Think about how you could rearrange the tiles to form a different solution.

- Look for other solutions. If you find any, record them, too.

- Be ready to explain the decisions you made.

The Bigger Picture

Thinking and Sharing

Ask pairs to check their squares to be sure that they follow the conditions of all three rules. Then, have them post their work.

Use prompts such as these to promote class discussion:

- What strategies did you use to arrange your tiles?

- Did you ever get "stuck"? If so, how did you get "unstuck"?

- How could you be sure that your design followed all three rules?

- Do you see any patterns in your design? Describe them.

- Which other squares are exactly like yours? Which are different? How are they different?

Writing

Have children tell what they could do to change their square into a new square that also follows all the rules.

Extending the Activity

Challenge children to make a 4-by-4 square using four different colors of Color Tiles in each row, column, and diagonal. Have them follow this rule: *No two of the same colors may touch along a side, but they may touch at a corner.*

Where's the Mathematics?

Children may initially apply a trial-and-error approach to finding the solution to this activity. Later, they may use transformational geometry by flipping certain arrangements to bring them into compliance with the rules. They may also find that a formation that does not work might do so if they rotated it and flipped some of its parts.

This activity presents a good opportunity for children to practice and expand their math vocabulary as they use such words as *row, column, horizontal, vertical,* and *diagonal.*

Some pairs may use the strategy of following the rules for the formation of the square in the order given, analyzing their results each time, and amending them if necessary. For example, suppose a pair created the following arrangement in response to the first two rules given in *On Their Own.* (The square must have 4 of each color of tile; no 2 tiles of the same color may touch along a side.)

R	G	B	Y
B	Y	R	G
G	R	Y	B
Y	B	G	R

While the arrangement satisfies the first two rules, it does not satisfy the third rule (No 2 tiles of the same color may touch at a corner). Once this is recognized, the pair might rearrange tiles in the third and fourth rows as shown.

R	G	B	Y
B	Y	R	G
R	G	B	Y
B	Y	R	G

In making the foregoing change, however, the fourth rule (The order of the colors in each row must differ from the order in every other row) is violated in the creation of two pairs of identical rows. If children notice that the columns all have different color sequences, they may rotate the arrangement one-quarter turn to the right so that the color sequences of the columns become the color sequences of the rows, thus getting the solution shown on the next page:

B	R	B	R
Y	G	Y	G
R	B	R	B
G	Y	G	Y

Once they have found such a solution, children may be surprised at the number of patterns. For example, the solution shows blue-red repeated in the first row, yellow-green in the second, red-blue in the third, and green-yellow in the fourth. In addition, the two-color pattern in the first row is reversed in the third row, and the two-color pattern in the second is reversed in the fourth row. Children who see that the first and third rows have only blue and red and that the second and fourth rows have only yellow and green may be able to find more solutions by making these rearrangements: Exchange the first and third rows; exchange the second and fourth rows; exchange the first and second rows and the third and fourth rows.

Children who go on to try to make the 4-by-4 square in which like colors may touch at a corner may reach this solution:

Y	G	R	B
B	R	G	Y
G	Y	B	R
R	B	Y	G

Further scrutiny of this solution reveals interesting patterns.

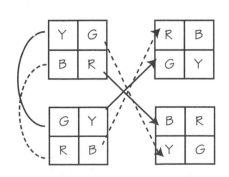 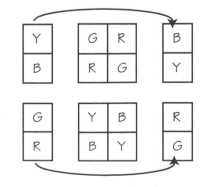

TILE MASTERS

Getting Ready

What You'll Need

Color Tiles, 6 each of red, yellow, and blue per group

Books or heavy folders to serve as barriers, 1 per group

3 x 3 Color Tile grids, 1 per child, page 96

Overhead Color Tiles and/or Color Tile grid paper transparency (optional)

Overview

In this game for four players, children take turns building secret Color Tile arrangements according to given criteria. Then they ask questions in order to discover the arrangements made by others. In this activity, children have the opportunity to:

◆ create tile arrangements that satisfy specific conditions

◆ build spatial visualization skills

◆ develop questioning strategies

The Activity

You may want to model various arrangements of three tiles of a color to show how they may touch along a complete side.

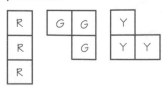

In preparation for the game, you may want to demonstrate how the "Tile Masters" may hide their secret square from the other players behind a stack of books.

Introducing

◆ Build and display this 3-by-3 Color Tile square.

◆ Call on volunteers to describe your square. Then record this description of it on the chalkboard:

1. *It is a 3-by-3 square made up of Color Tiles.*

2. *It has 3 red, 3 yellow, and 3 blue tiles.*

3. *Every tile of one color touches another tile of that same color along a complete side.*

◆ Now ask children to make a different 3-by-3 square that follows the same description as your square.

◆ Have several volunteers display their squares. Have the class check that each square follows the same description.

R	R	R
B	Y	Y
B	B	Y

On Their Own

Play *Tile Masters!*

Here are the rules:

1. This is a game for 4 players. The object is to guess the Tile Masters' secret square by asking as few questions as possible.

2. Players decide who will be the 2 Tile Masters and who will be the 2 Guessers.

3. The Tile Masters work together using 9 Color Tiles—3 red, 3 yellow, and 3 blue—to build a secret square according to this rule: *Each tile must touch another tile of the same color along a full side.*

4. The Guessers try to guess the square by asking questions that have "yes" or "no" answers.

5. The Tile Masters answer the questions and keep track of how many are asked.

6. The Guessers use the Tile Masters' answers to try to make a square that matches the secret square.

7. The game ends when the Guessers' square matches the secret square.

- Play several games of *Tile Masters*. Take turns being a Tile Master and a Guesser.

- Be ready to talk about the kinds of questions that were helpful and those that were not.

The Bigger Picture

Thinking and Sharing

Invite children to talk about their games and describe some of the thinking they did.

Use prompts like these to promote class discussion:

- When you were a Tile Master, how did you and the other Tile Master decide what square to build?

- What was the greatest number of questions the Guessers needed to guess the square? What was the smallest number?

- When you were a Guesser, what kind of questions were most helpful in matching the squares? What kind of questions were least helpful?

- If you played *Tile Masters* again, would you ask different kinds of questions than you asked before? Why?

Writing

Have children explain how the questions they asked in their last game were different from those they asked in their first game.

Extending the Activity

1. Have children play a version of *Tile Masters* in which the aim is to get as many points as possible. Instead of asking "yes/no" questions, Guessers ask "Is it—?" and "What's in—?" questions. For each "Is it—?" question that is guessed correctly, the Guessers get a point. If the guess is incorrect, the Tile Masters get a point. For all "What's in—?" questions asked, the Tile Masters get a point.

Teacher Talk

Where's the Mathematics?

Children who assume the role of Tile Masters will likely realize that part of their challenge in creating a secret square is to make one that is different from those previously made. As they assume the role of Guessers, children should begin to understand the importance of phrasing their questions so as to elicit the greatest amount of information possible from a single "yes" or "no" answer.

In both the roles of Tile Master and Guesser, players need to depend on everyone's clear understanding of the meaning of location words. Most children will be able to use *top, bottom, right, left,* and *middle* correctly, but some will need to be reminded how to differentiate between *row* and *column.*

There are only two possible basic arrangements of tiles. Any other arrangement is merely a flip or rotation of one of these two configurations. The numbers represent the three colors.

Arrangement 1

1	1	1
2	2	2
3	3	3

Arrangement 2

1	1	1
2	2	3
2	3	3

Either preceding the first game or after playing several games, some children may devise a way of numbering or lettering their square outlines to make it easier for the Tile Masters and Guessers to communicate about the locations of the tiles. Here are some sequences that groups have used:

1	2	3
4	5	6
7	8	9

A	B	C
D	E	F
G	H	I

T1	T2	T3
M1	M2	M3
B1	B2	B3

2. Have children play *Tile Masters* again, this time using a 4-by-4 square made from sixteen Color Tiles, four each of all four colors.

Some Guessers may keep track of their questions and their responses as they try to build their secret square. (Doing this has the added advantage of helping Guessers to avoid repeating previously asked questions.) One group of Guessers recorded their first questions this way:

Question Asked	Answer	What I Learned
1. Is the top left tile yellow?	No	The top left tile isn't yellow.
2. Is the top left tile blue?	No	The top left tile isn't blue, so the top left tile must be red.

As children continue to play, they may discover ways to get more than one bit of information from a single question. For example, the Guessers whose work is above could have learned that the top left tile is red by asking the single question, "Is the top left tile yellow or blue?" instead of asking both questions 1 and 2. Once having discovered the color of the top left tile, the Guessers had an idea about possible locations of the other two red tiles, since all tiles of a color must touch along a complete side.

As children continue to play the game, they may discover the advantages of starting their questioning about the color of the tile in one of the corner boxes. This is because a corner box joins only two other boxes, whereas other boxes each join three or four other boxes. So, determining the colors of tiles that join a corner box takes the least number of questions.

Product	Numbers rolled
1	
2	
3	
4	
5	
6	
7	
8	
9	
10	
11	
12	

Product	Numbers rolled
13	
14	
15	
16	
17	
18	
19	
20	
21	
22	
23	
24	

Product	Numbers rolled
25	
26	
27	
28	
29	
30	
31	
32	
33	
34	
35	
36	